WORLDWIDE GUIDE TO
NAKED PLACES

COMPILED BY THE EDITORS OF NAKED MAGAZINE

7th Edition

Published by The Nazca Plains Corporation
Las Vegas, Nevada
2010

ISBN: 978-1-935509-71-4

Published by

The Nazca Plains Corporation ®
Las Vegas NV 89109-8000

Cover, Wei Keong and Vladislav Gansovsky
Art Director, Blake Stephens

YEP... YOU'VE FOUND IT!

THE authority on gay, naked travel

WORLDWIDE!

Naked Magazine and The Nazca Plains Corporation are proud to bring you the very latest edition of the most complete guide to gay naked travel in the world. We've tried our best to make this the most complete, up to date and current guide to places known to have a gay naked following. The one thing that makes this guide so special is that it's specifically geared to the gay naked traveler-namely YOU! Although being naked is for those using this guide, just remember that people, places and naked status change VERY quickly. So, if you find a B&B (gay bed and breakfast, for those uninformed) or location that's gone clothed, drop us a line and let us know. This guide is only as good as the info we put in it, so help us help you and keep us informed! The form on the opposite page can be mailed directly to the Naked Magazine's home offices, or you speed things up and drop us an email at **NakedMagazine@aol.com.**

Remember – anyone can get naked...

it's up to you to stay NAKED!

We Need You!

Please send us any information that you may have about any new and/or improved gay clothing-optional accommodations, beaches, camp grounds, activities, or organizations. You'll help make the next edition of Worldwide Guide to Naked Places more useful to your fellow naked enthusiasts by filling out and sending us the following updates. ANY information you can provide is appreciated. By no means do you need to complete all sections!

Please note any correction(s) to a current listing or information about a potential new listing.

_____

_____

_____

Location including name, address, phone number, toll-free number, fax, Email, and Website if it is an accommodation, activity operator or organization

_____

_____

_____

Description of the nude beach, recreation area such as running trail or hot springs, organization, resort, guesthouse, charter operation or tour operator:

_____

_____

_____

Description of the facilities, area, activity - with special attention to its greatest assets and uniqueness:

_____

_____

_____

Directions to the accommodation, facility or area - particularly if it is a beach, recreational area, or camping facility off the beaten path:

_____

_____

_____

Please use additional sheets of paper for more information, if necessary.

Mail to:
    Naked Magazine
    PO Box 27432
    Austin, TX 78755

Email to:
    NakedMagazine@aol.com

CONTENTS

USA

ALABAMA   4

ALASKA   7

ARIZONA   9

ARKANSAS   14

CALIFORNIA (NORTHERN)   16

CALIFORNIA (SOUTHERN)   28

COLORADO   44

CONNECTICUT   47

DELAWARE   48

DISTRICT OF COLUMBIA   49

FLORIDA   51

GEORGIA   70

HAWAII   72

ILLINOIS   80

INDIANA   81

IOWA   82

KANSAS   84

KENTUCKY   85

LOUISIANA	86
MAINE	89
MARYLAND	91
MASSACHUSETTS	92
MICHIGAN	98
MINNESOTA	100
MISSOURI	102
NEBRASKA	105
NEVADA	106
NEW HAMPSHIRE	109
NEW JERSEY	110
NEW MEXICO	114
NEW YORK	117
NORTH CAROLINA	123
OHIO	124
OKLAHOMA	126
OREGON	128
PENNSYLVANIA	130
RHODE ISLAND	132
SOUTH CAROLINA	133
SOUTH DAKOTA	135
TENNESSEE	137
TEXAS	139
UTAH	147

VERMONT   148

VIRGINIA   151

WASHINGTON   152

WEST VIRGINIA   155

WISCONSIN   156

UNITED STATES TERRITORIES

PUERTO RICO   160

US VIRGIN ISLANDS   161

INTERNATIONAL

AUSTRALIA   164

AUSTRIA   177

BARBADOS   179

BRAZIL   180

CANADA   181

CARIBBEAN ISLANDS   194

COSTA RICA   197

DENMARK   199

FINLAND   201

FRANCE   203

GERMANY   207

GREECE   213

ICELAND   217

INDONESIA	218
IRELAND	219
ISRAEL	221
ITALY	222
MEXICO	227
NETHERLANDS	230
NEW ZEALAND	231
NORWAY	236
PORTUGAL	238
RUSSIA	241
SOUTH AFRICA	242
SPAIN	245
SWEDEN	253
SWITZERLAND	255
THAILAND	256
UNITED KINGDOM	257

INTRODUCTION

Let's face it... getting naked in public isn't always easy and it's even tougher to STAY naked in some situations, but thanks to this guide, we try to make it a little easier to find those 'special spots' where one can bank on the fact that "less is more." Here are a few pointers that will make life easier for the gay naked traveler:

- Not familiar with the area? Try finding commonplace on the web by corresponding with other gay nudists in the area. Still not finding what you're looking for? The local club will be glad to assist you with the local information. It's bound to produce results!

- In some situations it's good to be a follower: If others aren't naked in a certain spot, you shouldn't be either (unless you're in the cast of 'Hair' or 'Oh, Calcutta'... but we digress). Go with the flow and use good common sense when disrobing.

- Just because a guy is naked, doesn't necessarily mean he is looking for more than a little sun. Respect the people around you. If two people want to hook up, so be it, but if a fella is simply looking to get naked simply to get naked, keep a distance. Don't ruin the experience for everyone just because the Viagra kicked in...

- Sex. Now that we've got your attention... Golden Rule: If you MUST romp while in the buff, please don't do it in public. This is the major reason the nudist community is cracked down on. Like we said above, don't ruin it for everyone else for selfish reasons. If you value time away from jail and embarrassment, keep the mouse in the house kids. It keeps things so MUCH simpler.

- Give a hoot, don't pollute! Leave things CLEANER than how you found them. Set the good example and keep your area tidy!

- Be careful to read ALL signage: meaning, if a sign prohibits alcohol, nudism, fireworks or wearing white shoes after Labor Day, then adhere to it!

- This isn't a National Geographic expedition, so leave the camera at home. Taking unsolicited pictures of other nudists is just plain tacky.

- Co-exist peacefully with fellow CLOTHED sun bathers. Just because someone doesn't want to bare it all does not mean you have a right to harass them. Just remember, they're like you... only clothed!

- It's up to you to enforce such rules while on the beach, so if you see something fishy (and we don't mean of the carp variety) stand up for what you believe in and say something to stop it. Don't let one person ruin it for hundreds of others.

- The simple fact is, we've always been told that what counts is the beauty found on the inside, but let's face it... we all know that's not necessarily true in most situations. Just remember that people come in all shapes and sizes, and that a smile on your face with a great attitude is usually enough to make ANYONE feel comfortable, naked or not. Accept each other's differences and embrace diversity in body, mind and value. It's not always about the perfectly defined abs or the well-sculpted arms when being a gay nudist. It's about feeling free. So, drop the predispositions (your pants as well) and let it all hang loose because ultimately, that's what it's all about. Anyone can get naked... it's up to you to STAY NAKED!

UNITED STATES

OF AMERICA

ALABAMA

NUDE CLUBS / GROUPS / ORGANIZATIONS

DRUID CITY NUDIST CLUB (DCNC)

5042 Pinewood Lane
Tuscaloosa, AL 35404-4751
(205) 507-4611
Email: druidnudes@home.com - bamaroy2@aol.com

Monthly newsletters
1 party per month (fee)
Events include: beaches, camp/cook-outs at gay campgrounds, swim parties
Free self-JPGs for attendees.

BIRMINGHAM AREA DANGLERS - BAD BOYS

(205) 991-0104
Contact Greg for more info.

Members only newsletter
Unlimited attendance
Potential members welcome
Minimum one gathering a month

CLOTHING-OPTIONAL ACCOMMODATIONS

BLACK BEAR CAMP

10565 US Highway 280W
PO Box 210
Waverly, AL 36879
(334) 887-5152
Email: john@blackbearcamp.net
Website: www.blackbearcamp.net

A campground for men only offering no restrictions on nudity. Pool, hot tub. Bunk rooms and campsites available.

SPRING CREEK CAMPGROUND

163 Campground Road
Geneva, AL 36340
(334) 684-3891
Fax: (334) 684-8809
Email: info@springcreekcampground.net
Website: www.springcreekcampground.net

Campground mostly for gay men. 14 cabins, 42 campsites. Nudity permitted throughout. Pool. One hour to Florida panhandle beaches.Open all year.

ALABAMA

NUDE BEACHES / RECREATION AREAS

BON SECOUR NATIONAL WILDLIFE REFUGE (NEAR GULF SHORES, AL)

Nestled in the Alabama Coastline, this pristine windswept coastal barrier on the Fort Morgan Peninsula is a refuge protecting over 6,000 acres of untouched natural terrain. The still waters of the bay lead inland to salt marshes, which feed rare cypress swamps. Inland dunes are home to a forest of evergreens, Live Oaks and Pine covered in Spanish moss. Hikers will enjoy the views from many miles of available trails and naturalists will find peaceful tranquility in this rare and fascinating ecosystem. Our latest report states that there have been arrests for nude sunbathing. Apparently risk is low as the area is not heavily patrolled. As always, use your best judgment before disrobing.

DIRECTIONS: Take Route 59 to Gulf Shores. Right on Highway 180 west (Fort Morgan Road) for almost 9 miles, past the 12-mile marker, and turn left on unmarked dirt road (just at the "Real Estate" billboard, "Dune Lakes East Boundary," with a power substation on your right after you have turned). Parking is limited, so arrive early. Walk west down the beach for a mile before disrobing.

ALASKA

CLOTHING-OPTIONAL ACCOMMODATIONS

AURORA WINDS

7501 Upper O'Malley
Anchorage, AK 99516
(907) 346-2533 or (800) 642-9640
FAX: (907) 346-3192
EMAIL: awbnb@alaska.net

NUDE BEACHES / RECREATION AREAS

NANCY LAKE RECREATION AREA
(NEAR HOUSTON, AK)

This 22,685-acre park lies east of the Susitna west of the Talkeetna Mountains and is known primarily for its outdoor recreation. Lynx Lake Loop, an eight mile chain of lakes, is most famous for canoeing. This tranquil setting is home to hundreds of lakes, which host fishing and all manner of water sports. Unspoiled forests provide trails for camping and hiking. Nancy Lake State Recreation Area is 90 minutes north of Anchorage. Private cabins are available for overnight or weekend stays.

DIRECTIONS: North on Route 1 from Anchorage to Parks Highway (#3). Past the town of Houston, at mile 67 on the left, is the Nancy Lake Parkway. The canoe trailhead is clearly posted about 5 miles into the recreation area.

STORMY LAKE
(ANCHORAGE, AK)

Part of Captain Cook State Recreation Area, Stormy Lake is located on the Kenai Peninsula, just 25 miles north of Kenai. Whether canoeing, fishing or hiking, nature watching is key. Many of the natural species that inhabit this area include: bears, moose, coyotes, wolves, Beluga whales, harbor seals, bald eagles, sandhill cranes and trumpeter swans.

DIRECTIONS: From Anchorage, take route 1 south to Kenai and take the spur road north for 26 miles to Stormy Lake.

UNALASKA ISLAND

Remote Unalaska Island is both an archaeological and botanical site. Pick berries or take a marine tour. The island offers fishing, hiking, biking, kayaking, wildlife viewing, and a most beautiful and popular skinny-dipping lake nestled in a hidden valley. Warm in July and August, the lake has a fine sandy bottom.

DIRECTIONS: Drive to the top of General's Hill and park. Hike 1/2 mile to the first lake and another 1/8 mile to the second lake.

ARIZONA

NUDE CLUBS / GROUPS / ORGANIZATIONS

ARIZONA NUDE DUDES (ANDES)

PO Box 32776
Phoenix, AZ 85064-2776
Hotline: (602) 817-6907
Email: andes@swlink.net - info@aznudedudes.org
Website: www.aznudedudes.org

Approx. 100 members
Members-only newsletter
Yearly dues: $20 single / $30 couple
Limited attendance per host
Potential members welcome
6 parties per month (fee)

Check our Website for a list of events for the month
Events include: indoor/outdoor, potluck, pool/hot tub, movie nights, theme/
holiday, dance, exercise/aerobics, hiking, hot springs, river/beach, house
boating/canoeing, game nights, theatre

TUCSON TANNERS

PO BOX 84
Cortaro, AZ 85652-0084
(520) 742-6731
Email: TucsonNude@aol.com
Website: www.nakedplanet.org/tt_guidelines.html

CLOTHING-OPTIONAL ACCOMMODATIONS

ARIZONA ROYAL VILLA RESORT

4312 N. 12th Street
Phoenix, AZ 85014
(888) 266-6884
(602) 266-6883
Email: info@royalvilla.com
Website: www.royalvilla.com

Ground floor desert styled private resort apartments/ suites for gay men. 19 units, from small hotel rooms to one bedroom apartments. Close (walk) to local bars. All rooms with full accommodations.

Satellite TV, Showtime and HBO. Nudity Permitted. Nature trails and day passes for non-guests for nude sunbathing 10 AM – 5 PM, $10. Free high speed internet, restaurants, baths. Pool, hot tub, outdoor shower, nature train, gyms close by. Phoenix's biggest and longest running men's place to stay and play.

ARIZONA SUNBURST INN

6245 N. 12th PL
Phoenix, AZ 85014
(800) 974-1474
(602) 274-1474
Email: Wayne@azsunburst.com
Website: www.azsunburst.com

All male bed & breakfast resort that caters to nudists; open all year. Private yard, heated pool and spa. Centrally located, close to bars. Queen size beds with TV/ VCR in each room. Free local calls. Stay 6 nights and 7th is free.

LARRY'S BED & BREAKFAST

502 W. Claremont Ave.
Phoenix, AZ 85013-1309
(602) 249-2974
Email: kenezz1@cox.net

European style Bed & Breakfast in quite residential neighborhood catering to gay men and women. Pool, patio and hot tub. Nudity permitted everywhere. Open yearround. 1 double with private bath; 2 doubles with shared bath. Many repeat guests.

TORTUGA ROJA BED & BREAKFAST

2800 E. River Rd.
Tucson, AZ 85718
(800) 467-6822
(520) 577-6822
Email: redtrtl@tortugaroja.com
Website: www.tortugaroja.com

Bed & Breakfast for gay men and women. Desert setting on 4 acres. Hot tub. Nude sunbathing.

ARIZONA

NUDE BEACHES / RECREATION AREAS

SYCAMORE CREEK
(NEAR MESA AZ)

About an hour from Metropolitan Phoenix, this site offers spectacular hiking through agiant saguaro cactus forest, towering canyons, various swimming holes and creekside sunning. Water is abundant except during late summer. Easy hike, shoes recommended.

> *DIRECTIONS:* From Phoenix, take State Rd 87 (Beeline Highway) about 23 miles north from Shea Blvd. A half mile past marker 212, turn right onto the dirt road before the bridge. Follow the road to an old concrete creek crossing. Four wheel drive vehicles recommended beyond this point. Park or 4WD north across the bridge and up the trail about 1/4 mile. Turn left at large pink river rock. Follow side path to ledge. Climb down uneven step trail approximately 100 feet to swimming hole.

GORDON CREEK
(NEAR PAYSON, AZ)

In the Tonto National Forest, Gordon Creek is at the base of the Mogollon Rim. Clear water runs most of the year, stopping in June. Best time to go is in late spring or early fall. Portions of the road are rough and narrow, drive cautiously. Not recommended for tall vehicles or motor-homes. Several areas of the creek are open for exploration, hiking, swimming and jumping off rocks.

> *DIRECTIONS:* From Payson, go east on State Rd. 260 about 20 miles to Christopher Creek. Continue about 3 miles; turn right on Colcord Rd. (Forest Rd. 291). Go about 4 miles to Forest Rd. 200. Turn right on FR 200 and travel about 6-1/2 miles to a turnoff after descending a long hill (look for Trail 178 on the right). Turn right and follow the dirt road about 1/2 mile to the camping area.

TANQUE VERDE FALLS - REDDINGTON PASS (NEAR TUCSON, AZ)

East of the Rincon Mountains in Arizona's cattle country is Tanque Verde Falls. When the water is running at its fullest, the crashing force into this narrow granite canyon is something to behold. Be sure you have a good grip on something when viewing up close? The rocks can be slippery and very dangerous.

DIRECTIONS: From I-10, take Grant Rd east until road intersects with Tanque Verde Rd. on the eastern end of Tucson. Turn east onto Tanque Verde Rd. and follow road for many miles. Tanque Verde Rd. turns into Reddington Rd. which becomes a dirt road. Follow dirt road up mountainside about two miles. Look for signs saying "Upper Tanque Verde Falls." Park along dirt road and take trail to sandy beach surrounded by large boulders in canyon. Nude hiking/ sunbathing begins here. Follow canyon up to wire fence (about 1-1/2 miles) for beautiful scenery and deep swimming holes.

ARIZONA

ARKANSAS

NUDE CLUBS / GROUPS / ORGANIZATIONS

ARKANSAS NATURISTS

PO BOX 3695
Fayetteville, AR 72702-3695
Email: ArkNats@aol.com - Terrycolp@excite.com

CENTRAL ARKANSAS NUDISTS (CAN)

13801 Barth Rd
Alexander, AR 72002
Contact: Tommy Tedder (501) 847-1918
Email: natsnat@aol.com

NATURAL STATE NATURISTS (NSN)

PO Box 492
Avoca, AR 72711-0492
(479) 451-8066
Email: sugbrsdn@mc2k.com - nudetrdrvr@aol.com
Website: http://groups.yahoo.com/group/naturalStateNaturists

NUDE BEACHES / RECREATION AREAS

FLAT ROCK
(FAYETTEVILLE, AR)

One quarter mile of huge rock formations on the White River. Also known as "Thompson's Cut," "Screech Hole," and "Slippery Rock." A beautiful area offering secluded spots for sunbathing. Bring plenty of water because the rocks can get hot! Also, we've heard you need to stay away from the trail on the south side of the river - the farmer who owns the property can get testy and may have you prosecuted for trespassing.

DIRECTIONS: Take State Route 16 past Durham. When you enter Madison County, take the first road to the left and follow it across the river to the metal gate (don't block the gate or park in road). After the gate, walk through two pastures (upstream direction) to the foot bridge leading to rocks. Neighbors are not thrilled about nude use of Flat Rock - so it's best not to ask them for directions if you get lost.

CALIFORNIA (NORTHERN)

NUDE CLUBS / GROUPS / ORGANIZATIONS

BARE BUNS CALIFORNIA (BBC)

PO Box 34361
San Diego, CA 92163
(619) 239-NUDE (6833)
Email: info@BarebunsCalifornia.org
Website: www.barebunscalifornia.org

BARELY SOCIAL

PO Box 700864
San Jose, CA 95170-0864
Email: nathan@bothner.com
Website: www.geocities.com/westhollywood/village/1713

One event per month (fee)
Summer beach trips

BAYSIDE BARE BOYS (BBB)

PO Box 5402
San Jose, CA 95150-5402
Email: bareboys@ebold.com
Website: www.geocities.com/westhollywood/6950

BOYZ IN THE WOODZ CLUB (BWCLUB)

San Francisco, CA
Email: RJ@BWClub.net
Website: www.BWClub.net

Average attendance 6
No dues, no rules, just for fun!
Weekly San Rafael Sunday brunch followed by a hike to a nude beach or lake

CALIFORNIA MEN ENJOYING NATURISM (C-MEN)

8424-A Santa Monica blvd #119
West Hollywood, CA 90069
(877) 683-4781
Email: wehojohn2aol.com - info@cmen.info
Website: www.cmen.info

CALIFORNIA NUDE WORKOUT (CNW)

(818) 779-0909
Email: buffworkout@hotmail.com

FRATERNITY LOS ANGELES (FRATERNITY LOS ANGELES)

8424A Santa Monica BLVD, Suite 285
West Hollywood, CA 90069
(310) 652-4475
Email: FratLA@aol.com

LET IT ALL HANG OUT (LIAHO)

PO Box 1508
San Anselmo, CA 94979-1508
Email: LIAHONaturists@aol.com
Website: www.LIAHO.org

LONG BEACH AREA NUDE DUDES (L'BAND)

PO Box 1565
Long Beach, CA 90801-1565
(888) 487-9025 Ext 1002 or (310) 884-1019
Email: lband@altern.org
Website: www.lband.beach-cities.com

LOS ANGELES NEDE GUYS (LANG)

8424-A Santa Monica Blvd, PMB #249
West Hollywood, CA 90069
(818) 787-LANG (5264)
Email: clubla@clublang.com
Website: www.clublang.com

MALES AU NATUREL SACRAMENTO (MANS)

PO Box 19601
Sacramento, CA 95819-0601
Email: NakedGeno@yahoo.com
Website: www.mans-ca.com/index.html

PALM SPRINGS SOCIAL SUN TANNERS (PSSST)

PO Box 767
Palm Springs, CA 92263-0767
(760) 325-5815
Email: nakedpssst@yahoo.com - pssst4u@aol.com

SACRAMENTO AREA NUDISTS FOR GAY MEN (SANS)

PO Box 189573
Sacramento, CA 95818-9573
Email: armo@pacbell.net

Approx 50 members Members-only newsletter
Yearly dues: $25.00 single / couple
Potential members welcome
1-2 events per month (fee)
Events include: indoor/outdoor, potluck, pool/hot tub, movie night, theme/holiday, river/beach

SAN FRANCISCO KINDRED NUDISTS (SKINS)

PO Box 14544
San Francisco, CA 94114-0544
Email: skins@gay.com
Website: www.skins.cc

Approx 65 members
Public newsletter
Yearly dues: $20 single / $35 couple
Limited attendance
Potential members welcome
1-2 parties per month (no fee)
Events Included: movie nights, potluck, theme/holiday, house-boating/canoeing.

CLOTHING-OPTIONAL ACCOMMODATIONS

EAGLE'S PEAK

PO Box 750
Forestville, CA 95436
(877) 891-6466
(707) 887-9218
Fax: (707) 887-9219
Email: info@eaglespeak.net
Website: www.eaglespeak.net

A private vacation home that sleeps 4, for men only. There are 2 campsites available that must be booked by the same group in the house. Nudity permitted with no restrictions. 26 acres, hot tub, sun deck. Reservations required.

HIGHLANDS RESORT

CALIFORNIA - NORTHERN

1400 Woodland Dr.
(Mail: PO Box 346)
Guerneville, CA 95446
(707) 869-0333
Fax (707) 869-0370
Email: muffins@HighlandsResort.com
Website: www.highlandsresort.com

Resort for gay men and gay women. Nudity permitted at swimming pool and spa areas. 16 rooms; 10 with private baths.

RUSSIAN RIVER RESORT (TRIPLE "R")

16390 4th St.
PO BOX 2419
Guerneville, CA 95446
(800) 41-resort
(707) 869-0691
Fax (707) 869-0698
Email: info@russianriverresort.com
Website: www.russianriverresort.com

A resort that caters to gay men, and some women, with nudity in the hot tub area.

NUDE BEACHES / RECREATION AREAS

AMERICAN RIVER
(NEAR AUBURN, CA)

As much as 50 miles of the north and middle forks of the American River run through the Auburn State Recreation Area which also offers 50 miles of hiking and horseback trails. In addition to whitewater rafting (the main attraction), there is fishing and camping, but be sure to bring everything you need. Concessions are few. This is real wilderness country.

> *DIRECTIONS:* Take I-80 east to the Elm Ave. exit. Drive east on Elm Ave. Turn left on Highway 49 (High St.). Go about two miles to an area where there is parking space on both sides of the road. Look for the trail heading toward the river. Take the trail down for a few minutes to where it intersects a very broad trail/dirt road. If you continue across the road and down, you'll reach the straight nude area. To get to the gay area, turn right on the wide trail/road and continue for a few minutes until you see a metal stake marking a trail to the left. Take that trail and continue downhill and then downstream for about 15 minutes. You will eventually reach a large rocky beach area. This is the beginning of the gay area, and continues for about ½ mile. Naked hiking along the river is common, as is naked sunbathing and swimming for the thick skinned (it's very cold water!).

ANGEL ISLAND
(NEAR SAN FRANCISCO, CA)

Angel Island, in San Francisco Bay, is a popular day trip. Located a mile from the Tiburon Peninsula, Angel Island is the largest island in San Francisco Bay. It is made up of grassy forest-covered hills covering 740 acres. During the summer, the fog reaches it later than most parts of the bay. Its tallest point is atop Mt. Livermore, which at 781 feet, provides spectacular views of the Golden Gate Bridge, San Francisco and beyond - fog permitting.

> *DIRECTIONS:* The Island is reached by State Park ferries. Perries Beach, which is clothing-optional, is a 45 minute walk from the dock.

BAKER BEACH
(SAN FRANCISCO, CA)

In San Francisco, Baker Beach is part of the Golden Gate National Recreation Area. The clothing-optional portion is found on its north end, just west of the Golden Gate Bridge's south end. The crowd is mixed - young and old, gay and straight. Great views of the city and harbor.

DIRECTIONS: Take Lincoln Blvd. to Bowley St. and then to Gibson Rd. At the west end of Gibson, walk toward the Golden Gate Bridge (north), down to the Beach, and then walk farther north to Baker Beach. The northern most lot offers the closest parking to the nude part of the beach.

BLACK SANDS BEACH — AKA BONITA BEACHES
(MARIN HEADLANDS, NEAR SAUSALITO, CA)

There are two main areas to Black Sands Beach; a large open beach and a series of smaller pocket beaches. The large beach is mostly nude and gay; the pocket beaches are almost entirely so.

DIRECTIONS: Take Highway 101 to Alexander Ave. exit. Turn left under the freeway and enter Marin Headlands on Conzelman Rd. Continue up the hill on Conzelman Rd. for 3-1/2 miles. Last winter's severe storms and surf severely damaged the vehicle access ramp and large portions of the parking area. The erosion has created sheer cliffs in these areas; however, the beach remains open to hikers via a rocky path to the south of the former parking area. Signs are posted directing visitors where to park along designated county roads near the beach.

To get to the very gay pocket beaches, take a fork off the main trail to the right, about 100 yards from where the main trail starts. Hike down about 10 minutes to the first of the smaller beaches. You usually have to dodge the surf to get around (or over) the rock formations that divide each beach. Be mindful of the tides throughout the day to make sure you don't get trapped at high tide in the late afternoon. An alternate route to one of the most popular of these pocket beaches is as follows: Drive about 1/8 mile beyond the former parking lot to a smaller parking area on the right side of the road, just before the old fortress ruins. Find the trail that starts at the end of a metal railing. It's a steep hike down the hill that takes about 10 minutes, but it's well worth the effort to visit these beaches!

BONNY DOON BEACH
(NORTH OF SANTA CRUZ, CA)

Bonny Doon Beach is located just north of Santa Cruz, CA and, weather permitting, is considered one of the most beautiful and accommodating spots for nudists in California. The beach is protected from wind by a repeating pattern of semicircle-shaped cliffs, but try to find a place a comfortable distance from the bottom, or watch for falling pebbles and smaller rocks. Sand dunes run along the south side of the beach and caves to the north. Crashing waves, strong currents, forceful riptides and unyielding undertows have made swimming here dangerous, so be very careful. Don't be surprised if you find a bevy of beach blanket party pals. This is a popular nudist spot and a great place to make friends. Dogs are welcome and whales are watched.

> *DIRECTIONS:* Bonny Doon beach is located at the intersection of Bonnie Doon Road and Hwy. 1, a mile south of Davenport Village, and about 10 miles northwest of Santa Cruz, at milepost 27.6. Find one of a few parking areas along Highway 1. The beach is located across the railroad tracks and down the hill.

BUTTE CREEK
(NEAR CHICO, CA)

Popular swimming holes for skinny dipping between Chico and Paradise. There is some sand for sunbathing. As always, be careful before disrobing if there are clothed bathers nearby.

> *DIRECTIONS:* Take CA-99 south from Chico, exit Skyway Road. Go east to Humbug Road and look for parked cars before you reach Honey Run Road. Park and walk to the creek or continue past Honey Run to a second site. There is a third site attainable via Helltown Road. Turn left onto Helltown and park at the end. Walk down the road, cross the bridge, and then walk 1/4 mile on the path to the right.

CLEAR CREEK
(NEAR REDDING, CA)

Located approximately 20 minutes from downtown Redding, Clear Creak is part of Clear Lake and its system of dams. This area, known as French Gulch, became famous during California's gold rush era. Folks still pan in the creek. It is a quiet, peaceful area that hosts fishing and hiking.

> *DIRECTIONS:* From Redding, head west/southwest on Placer St. (I-16) toward Igo. Placer St. will become Placer Rd. Park near the bridge over Clear Creek and follow the trail on the left side of the creek.

DEVIL'S SLIDE
(NEAR SAN FRANCISCO, CA)

Known as "Edun Cove" and officially as "Grey Whale Cove," Devil's Slide, as it is most commonly referred, is the length of approximately 3 football fields bordered by hills at either end. The area is equipped for camping, complete with soda machines, barbecue pits and bathrooms. There is also a concession stand that sells hot dogs and snacks. Although this is a clothing-optional area, some prefer to wear suits. Weekdays see a higher gay population.

DIRECTIONS: From San Francisco, take Highway 1 south about 5 miles past Pacifica. Look for Devil's Slide, a large cliff that drops off to the sea. There is an unmarked road a mile or so north of Montara, which will take you to the parking lot. Park at the marked "Beach Parking" area.

GARRAPATA BEACH
(NEAR MONTEREY, CA)

For years, access to this beach was blocked by private property, but recently the State of California acquired the property and added it to their portfolio of state parks. Considered by many to be one of the nicest beaches in Monterey County, quiet coves and secret caves lie under imposing mountain cliffs which overlook a mile long ribbon of pristine white sand. The north end is gay.

DIRECTIONS: Take Highway 1 from Monterey south (through Carmel) about 9 miles past Rio Rd. At the bridge over the Garrapata River, look for a stone house above the cliff. Park just north of the bridge. You can get to the beach by descending the 20 foot cliff on dirt steps to the riverside.

ALT. DIRECTIONS: Take Highway 1 from Monterey south (through Carmel). At Rio Road (next to Crossroads Shopping Center), drive exactly 9.6 miles to an "unofficial" parking area along the road. If you cross Garrapata Creek Bridge, you have gone too far.

HAGMIER POND
(NEAR BOLINAS, CA)

California's most popular lake for nude recreation is located in the Point Reyes National Seashore area. Springtime is the best time to visit. While the water is too polluted to swim in, the area remains popular with gay men, largely due to the high natural forest which surrounds it and provides a natural barrier of privacy.

DIRECTIONS: From Bolinas, take Highway 1 north approximately 5 miles past Stinson Beach. Past Audubon Canyon Ranch, you'll see cars parked on both sides of the highway. The location is 1-1/2 miles north of the city limits where you'll see a "Dogtown Pottery" sign. (If you pass Dogtown, you've gone too far.) At the entrance, walk right across a meadow and you'll see Hagmier Pond. The rim of the Pond is fairly steep, so find sunbathing areas around the little dam there. Wading in the pond is a popular activity, but you may think twice before swimming in it because this area is used as a watering hole for animals and is not purified.

LAND'S END BEACH
(SAN FRANCISCO, CA)

This beach is only a quarter of a mile long, full of rocks and can be cold and windy. So what's the draw? Depending on how you look at it, there is the incredibly breathtaking view of the Golden Gate Bridge and the San Francisco Bay from Land's End Beach, or the notorious dunes, trails and shrubs. For the record, Lands End is part of the GGNRA where nudity is legal, but public sex is not. Rangers do patrol the area on foot and horseback.

DIRECTIONS: Drive to or take the city bus (Muni #38) to the Cliff House at the end of Geary Blvd. Then go north on Point Lobos Ave. to Marine Way to Seal Rocks State Beach.

ALT. DIRECTIONS: Park in the parking lot up the road from the Cliff House and walk down the trail at the farthest end of the lot. Walk about 150 yards until you get to the road, but stay to the left, or bring your golf clubs. Where the road starts to turn right, look to your left and see a stairway and dog/leash sign. Follow that stairway to a second stairway on your left and walk to the cove with the naked men.

RED ROCK BEACH
(MARIN COUNTY, NEAR SAN FRANCISCO, CA)

While many nude beaches have dedicated followings, Red Rock Beach devotees have developed their own sophisticated Website (www.redrockbeach.com), complete with news, features, satellite photos, up-to-the-minute weather, tide charts, galleries of regular inhabitants, a daily picture of the area, and updated beach information. Avid Frisbee, paddle ball and board game tournaments join rock climbing and whale watching as things to do on this very active beach.

DIRECTIONS: The beach is on Highway 1 at milepost 11.35. About 1/2 mile south of Stinson Beach (which is clothing only) at the intersection of Panoramic Highway (and several miles north of Muir Beach) is a dirt parking area on the ocean side of the road (a smaller lot exists on the mountain side). From the parking lot, there is a 1/4 mile walk down a trail (steep sometimes, but always kept in good shape). Watch out for poison oak. During low tides, it's quite possible to park at Stinson Beach and walk south around the rocks.

SAN GREGORIO BEACH
(SAN MATEO COUNTY)

It was during San Francisco's 1967's "Summer of Love" that San Gregorio earned the distinction of becoming California's (the United State's) first legal nude beach. After 30 years, there are parking lots, but no concessions or bathrooms. Pets are allowed, but overnight camping is not. The gay section has a number of hand-built driftwood enclosures which are claimed by early arrivals.

DIRECTIONS: Take Highway 1, 5 miles south of Half Moon Bay and look for the intersections of Hwy. 1 and 84. About 100 yards north of the intersection, on the beach side, is a dirt road leading to a white gate with the sign "Toll Road." Pay the $2 fee to park and walk down the trail to the beach. Gay folks generally tend to inhabit the north end of the beach, which itself is located just north of San Gregorio State Beach (clothed).

OUR LAST REPORT: San Gregorio is an expansive, well populated beach west of San Jose on the California Coast. Its proximity to San Francisco assures that there are lots of naked men to keep you entertained for hours. The approach is quite simple. Just north of the State Beach parking lot is a small dirt road. Follow it for about a quarter of a mile and you'll come upon a lawn with cars all parked neatly in rows. You'll also meet the attendant. He'll collect a few pennies from you for parking (its private property) and he'll also explain the local etiquette to you. Don't get naked until you get to the bottom of the trail. Families to the left, boys to the right. Pretty standard.

As we approached the beach we were struck by how large it was. We were also struck by all the driftwood that littered the beach. We're not just talking sticks here. There were logs all over the beach. And a good thing, too, for now we noticed that, even though the sun was shining, the wind was really blowing. Beachgoers use all the driftwood to create shelters along the base of the cliffs. Then they fly a piece of clothing from a stick so you know the shelter is occupied. We were told that it's bad manners to walk up and look in! When we arrived, all the shelters were taken. However, near the base of the cliffs the wind lets up and the sand is quite pleasant. Since this stretch of shore is so wide open, you don't have to step over towels just to find a place for yours. As mentioned, the beach isn't that far away from San Francisco, which means it isn't that far from afternoon fog either. So, just be sure to get there early on a sunny day and you'll have a great experience finding the perfect log shelter and then strolling naked up and down the beach to see what other treats the beach has to offer.

WOHLER BRIDGE
(NEAR GUERNEVILLE,SONOMA COUNTY, CA)

On the Russian River, this fresh water spot became popular in the 70's as a nudist mecca, but neighbor complaints have brought police attention, so keep a watchful eye out. The currents are strong, so swim/wade with caution and stay close to shore.

DIRECTIONS: Located 90 minutes from San Francisco, take Highway 101 north past Santa Rosa. Turn left on West River Rd. and then turn right on Wohler Rd. Park in the lot next to the bridge and walk to the sandy beach about 1 mile upstream.

YUBA RIVER — AKA SOUTH FORK
(NEAR GRASS ALLEY/NEVADA CITY. CA)

Fishing, camping, hiking, whitewater rafting and canoeing are all part of the fun on this recreational river. On the south fork there is a picturesque skinny-dipping area with mixed nudist use.

DIRECTIONS Take Route 49 northwest out of Auburn; at Grass Valley take Route 20 west for 8 miles to Pleasant Valley Rd. Turn left, go past Lake Wildwood, to south Yuba River. Cross the bridge and park on either side of the road. Walk on the dirt road toward the river and then upstream until you notice a dip in the road, about a 3-minute walk from where you were parked. Take footpath on the left, up a hill and walk for 7 minutes until you reach a flume grade. Follow the footpath upstream along the grade until you cross the French Correll Creek and pass the State Park boundary sign. Continue walking for about 2 minutes and look for a trail on the right going about 40-50 yards down to a sandy skinny-dipping/sunbathing area.

CALIFORNIA (SOUTHERN)

NUDE CLUBS / GROUPS / ORGANIZATIONS

BARE BUNS OF CALIFORNIA (BBC)

PO Box 34361
San Diego, CA 92163
(619) 239-NUDE (6833)
Email: info@barebunsCalifornia.com
Website: www.barebunscalifornia.org

CALIFORNIA MEN ENJOYING NATURISM (CMEN)

PO Box 42
Sun Valley, CA 91353-0042
(818) 771-0664
Approx. 50 members
Email: WEHOJOHN@aol.com
Website: www.cmen.info

FRATERNITY LOS ANGELES

8424A Santa Monica Blvd., Suite 285
West Hollywood, CA 90069
(310) 652-4475
Email: FratLA@aol.com

Approx. 450 members
Provides a venue for the interaction of gay and bisexual men who are into jacking off, nudity, exhibitionism and other forms of "safe" intimacy. Guests must accompany a member or arrangements must be made in advance to be placed on the door list for a club gathering. Members of other clubs may call or send Email to be placed on the door list.

LOS ANGELES NUDE GUYS (LANG)

8424-A Santa Monica Blvd PMB 249
West Hollywood, CA 90069
Hotline: (818) 787-LANG (5264)
Email: clubla@clublang.com
Website: www.clublang.com/

Approx. 335 members
Public newsletter
Yearly dues: $20 single / $25 couple
Potential members welcome
3 - 7 parties per month (fee)
Events include: indoor/outdoor, potluck, pool/hot tub, movie nights, theme/ holiday, hiking, hot springs, house boating/canoeing

PALM SPRINGS SOCIAL SUN TANNERS (PSSST)

PO Box 767
Palm Springs, CA 92263-0767
Hotline: (760) 325-5815
Email: PSSST4U@aol.com

Approx. 140 members Public newsletter Yearly dues Unlimited attendance Potential members welcome 2+ parties a month (fee for guests only)

CALIFORNIA - SOUTHERN

CLOTHING-OPTIONAL ACCOMMODATIONS

AMBIENTE INN & THE BLACK PALM

37112 Palo Verde Drive
Cathedral City CA 92234
(760) 770-1697 Fax: (760) 770-8756
           (866) 223-3700
Email: mail@ambienteinn.com

An Inn with a Fetish Edge.

ALL WORLDS RESORT

526 Warm Sands Dr
Palm Springs CA 92264
(800) 798-8781 (760) 323-7505
Fax: (760) 323-1055
Email: reservations@allworldsresort.com
Website: www.allworldsresort.com

Resort catering to gay males; clothing-optional throughout the resort. High Sexual Temperature rating! 44 newly renovated rooms! Pamper yourself in this clothing optional resort. Featuring a provocative nature walk, a complete adult video library, 4 crystal blue swimming pools, 1 hot tub with waterfall, and 3 Jacuzzis. Workout area, 3 adult cable stations and close to gay nightlife. Continental breakfast included.

BACCHANAL

589 Grenfall Road
Palm Springs, CA 92264
(800) 806-9059
(760) 323-0760
Fax: (760) 416-4107
Email: reservations@bacchanalresort.com
Website: www.bacchanal.net

Resort catering to gay males. Nudity permitted throughout. 8 rooms, pool, 9-man spa. Continental breakfast included.

CAMP PALM SPINGS

1466 N. Palm Canyon Drive
Palm Springs CA 92262
(800) 793-0063
(760) 322-2267
Fax (760) 323-7005
Email: camper69@aol.com
Website: www.camp-palm-springs.com

A resort hotel catering to gay men with nudity allowed anywhere. 28 rooms. Pool, spa, steam room, gym. Breakfast included.

CANYON CLUB HOTEL

960 N Palm Canyon Dr.
Palm Springs CA 92262
(877) 258-2887
(760) 322-2267
Fax (760) 778-8061
Email: info@canyonclubhotel.com
Website: www.canyonclubhotel.com

A resort catering to gay males with nudity permitted everywhere except lobby and gym. 32 rooms and suites. Steam room, sauna, and large pool. Cable TV, Internet access, fee parking, continental breakfast. Close to downtown.

CATHEDRAL CITY BOY'S CLUB

68-369 Sunair Rd
Cathedral City CA 92234
(800) 472-0836
(760) 324-1350
Fax (760) 328-0267
Email: ccbc@earthlink.net
Website: www.ccbc-gay-resort.com

A resort that caters to gay males, with nudity poolside and throughout. Pool, jacuzzi, steam, and sauna. 21 rooms/suites.

CENTURY PALM SPRINGS

598 South Grenfall Rd.
Palm Springs, CA 92264
(800) 475-5188
(760) 323-9966
Fax: (760) 323-9933
Email: info@centurypalmsprings.com
Website: www.CenturyPalmSprings.com

Guesthouse for gay men. Entire resort is clothing-optional. Eightrooms with private baths. Swimming pool and spa. Continental breakfast served weekend (Sat & Sun) and holidays. Under new ownership, with newly renovated landscape.

CHESTNUTZ

641 San Lorenzo Road
Palm Springs, CA 92264
(800) 621-6973
(760) 325-5269
Email: Chestnutz1@aol.com
Website: www.chestnutz.com

A resort catering to gays only with nudity allowed anywhere. 12 rooms with private baths. Concierge service. Full breakfast provided. Pool, Jacuzzi, and full gym.

DESERT PARADISE RESORT HOTEL

615 Warm Sands Dr
Palm Springs CA 92264
(800) 342-7635 - (760) 320-5650
Fax (760) 320-0273
Email: dparadise9@aol.com
Website: www.desertparadise.com

A hotel that caters to gay males, with nudity anywhere on the grounds. 14 rooms, 2 suites. Large pool, Jacuzzi, fireplace, outdoor shower, exercise gazebo, fire pit. King size beds, microwaves, refrigerators, coffee pots, irons. Continental breakfast daily. 15 closed circuit adult video channels.

DMITRI'S GUESTHOUSE

931 21st St.
San Diego, CA 92102
(619) 238-5547
Website: www.dmitrisguesthouse.net

A guesthouse catering to gay men with nudity allowed anywhere.

EL MIRASOL VILLAS

525 Warm Sands Dr
Palm Springs CA 92264
(800) 327-2985
(760) 327-5913
Fax (760) 325-1149
Email: info@elmirasol.com
Website: www.elmirasol.com

A resort hotel catering to gay males; clothing-optional throughout the property. 2 pools, hot tub, steam room, continental breakfast.

GROVE GUESTHOUSE

1325 N. Orange Grove Ave.
Los Angeles, CA 90046
(888) LA GROVE
(323) 876-7778
Fax: (323) 876-8887
Email: info@groveguesthouse.com
Website: www.groveguesthouse.com

Enjoy your own private luxurious villa in a perfect central location catering to gay males with nudity allowed anywhere. Separate bedroom, full kitchen, and wonderful private pool/spa in tropical setting.

HACIENDA AT WARM SANDS

586 Warm Sands Dr
Palm Springs CA 92264
(800) 359-2007
(760) 327-8111
Fax: (760) 778-7890
Email: info@thehacienda.com
Website: www.thehacienda.com

A resort that caters to gay males with nudity allowed poolside and throughout the property. 10 rooms (all suites), two pools, spa, luxurious SE Asian decor, breakfast and lunch included.

HELIOS

280 E Mel Ave
Palm Springs CA 92262
(877) 435-4677
Email: info@yourgayresort.com
Website: www.yourgayresort.com

An upscale men's resort with clothing-optional pool and Jacuzzi area. 11 Units, 2 King Studios, 1 Queen Suite (2 baths), 1 2-bed 2-bath apartment, 6 Queen Studios, and 1 Queen Guest Room. Continental breakfast included. Beautiful location. Pets welcome. Intimate yet fun. Upscale, not uptight. The best of amenities and service.

INNDULGE PALM SPRINGS

601 Grenfall Rd
Palm Springs CA 92264
(800) 833-5675
(760) 327-1408
Fax (760) 327-7273
Email: inndulge@ix.netcom.com
Website: www.inndulge.com

A guesthouse catering to gay males with nudity allowed anywhere. 17 rooms, 2 suites. Pool, whirlpool. Breakfast included.

INN EXILE

545 Warm Sands Dr
Palm Springs CA 92264
(800) 962-0186 - (760) 327-6413
Fax (760) 320-5745
Email: innexile@earthlink.net
Website: www.innexile.com

A resort catering to gay males with nudity allowed anywhere on the resort. 31 rooms, 4 pools, 2 whirlpools, steam room, gym, billiard room. Breakfast and lunch included.

LAS PALMAS HOTEL PALM SPRINGS

1404 North Palm Canyon Drive
Palm Springs, CA 92262
(866) 552-7272
(760) 327-6883
Fax: (760) 327-6881

Large sparkling pool, spacious, sunny deck, with spectacular mountain views. Clothing optional Jacuzzi and poolside sunbathing. Intimate 17 room inn for perfect romantic getaway. Colorful Moroccan-inspired décor.

SAN VICENTE INN WEST HOLLYWOOD

845 San Vicente Blvd
West Hollywood CA 90069
(800) 577-6915
(310) 854-6915
Fax (310) 289-5929
Email: info@thesanvicenteinn.com
Website: www.thesanvicenteinn.com

A resort catering to gay males with nudity allowed anywhere. 10 rooms, 10 suites, 10 apartments. Pool, hot tub, steam, and gym. Continental breakfast included.

SANTIAGO RESORT

650 San Lorenzo Rd
Palm Springs CA 92264
(800) 710-7729
(760) 322-1300
Fax (760) 416-0347
Email: santiagops@earthlink.com
Website: www.santiagoresort.com

A resort catering to gay males with nudity allowed anywhere on the grounds. 10 rooms, 14 suites. Pool, whirlpool.

TERRAZZO RESORT

1600 East Palm Canyon Drive
Palm Springs, CA 92264
(866) TERRZZO (837.7996)
(760) 778-5883
Fax: (760) 416-2200
Email: info@terrazzo-ps.com
Website: www.terrazzo-ps.com

Recipient of the Out & About "Editor's Choice" Award several years in a row. Intimate and relaxing 12-room, clothing optional gay men's hotel.

CALIFORNIA - SOUTHERN

TRIANGLE INN

555 San Lorenzo Rd
Palm Springs CA 92264
(800) 732-7555
(760) 322-7993
Email: triangleinnps@earthlink.net
Website: www.triangle-inn.com

A resort catering to gay males with nudity permitted everywhere. Continental breakfast; social hour in the afternoons. Bicycles, pool, Jacuzzi, and two sun decks. All rooms have TVs, VCRs, and stereos. Large gay adult video selection. 4 Bedroom house also available for day, weekend or monthly rental.

VISTA GRANDE/ATRIUM/MIRAGE/ AVALON

574 Warm Sands Drive
Palm Springs, CA 92264
(800) 669-1069
(760) 322-2404
FAX (760) 320-1667
Email: mirage4men@aol.com
Website: www.mirage4men.com

Four accommodations in one! Nude sunbathing, heated pool, spa, fireplaces, tropical garden. One- and two-bedroom suites, with 4 adult channels. Waterfall, lagoon, and continental breakfast.

NUDE BEACHES / RECREATION AREAS

BLACK'S BEACH
(LA JOLLA, CA - NEAR SAN DIEGO)

For almost 30 years Black's Beach has been one of the most popular and well known nude beaches in the country. The northern end is generally considered to be the gay section, but straights and gays seem to co-exist in harmony throughout the entire stretch of beach. In 1977 voters turned down a measure legalizing nudity by a slim margin, but arrests are still pretty much unheard of. In summer months, naked crowds can top 5,000 or more stretching over a mile up the beach. It has a kind of carnival-style atmosphere, with activities including body painting (a tradition at Black's), Frisbee/hackysack and sandcastle construction contests, volleyball, swimming and body surfing. On most days, peddlers hawk soft drinks and beer along the beach. Please stay out of the eco-sensitive areas.

DIRECTIONS: Take I-5 north from San Diego to Genessee Ave. exit. Go west on Genessee through the first light where Genessee becomes N. Torrey Pines Rd. Go 1/2 mile and turn right onto Torrey Pines Scenic Dr. At the sign for the glider port, turn left on the road leading to it. The parking area is 300 feet above the beach; look for a path leading to a steep set of rough stairs down to the beach.

ALT. DIRECTIONS: From downtown San Diego, take I-5 (San Diego Freeway) and exit at La Jolla Village Drive. Go west about 1/2 miles on Torrey Pines Rd. Make a right while looking for the entrance to the Salk Institute on your left, just past the college (UCSD). Find Torrey Pines Scenic Dr.

DEEP CREEK HOT SPRINGS
(NEAR VICTORVILLE, CA)

One of America's premiere nude springs, Deep Creek is so popular that some can't wait to get there and walk in naked. Natural hot springs flow into three separate water-carved flat rock pools of varying temperature. The natural landscape is beautiful and the views are magnificent. The hot springs and surrounding area provide the tranquility and relaxed setting, making the naturist experience complete. Many commune with the natural setting, taking nature walks and hikes. Visitors must leave by sunset or camp at adjacent Bowen Ranch.

DIRECTIONS: From Barstow, take the Bear Valley Cutoff from I-15. Follow Highway 15 south, past Victorville, to Hesperia. Take Main St. through Hesperia 7.4 miles. After the Silverwood Lake sign, turn left onto Rock Springs Rd., follow Rock Springs 2-1/2 miles and go left onto Kiowa Rd., continue 1/2 and go right onto Roundup Way. When Roundup becomes a dirt road (it's handy to have a 4WD vehicle here, for water run-off sometimes creates big potholes in the road), travel 1-1/2 miles and turn right onto an unmarked road. Follow it about 6 miles until you come to a chain blocking the road at a gate house. Toot your horn and someone from Bowen Ranch will come out to collect a parking fee. Ask for a trail map at the gate house. Park in the designated area.

(If you wish, this is where you may also camp. The campsites are nearly barren so bring everything with you.) Take the trail, which is about a two-mile hike down to the creek and hot springs. Pay attention to the trail markers; with dozens of trails, it's easy to get lost! At the creek, you'll see a little beach. Cross the creek and in the area of big rocks check for the first of the soaking pools. Be sure to allow yourself plenty of time to hike back up (1,200 ft) before it gets dark. Camping is not allowed at the hot springs. Bring plenty of sunscreen, food, and especially water. There are no facilities for provisions.

PIRATE'S COVE
(NEAR MALIBU, CA)

A small secluded spot just south of Zuma beach, this natural enclave was a day-tripper's dream. Police have turned it into a nudist nightmare when they began a crackdown, ticketing everyone for issues involving nudity to dogs off leashes. The area still flourishes as a nudist haven in their absence, however.

DIRECTIONS: From Los Angeles follow Highway 1 north past Malibu to Zuma Beach. Park in one of the beach lots and walk south along either the sand or the service road to the cove. Climb over the rocks and find this small cove nestled under the cliffs.

EL MATADOR BEACH
(NEAR MALIBU, CA)

In 1984, the state combined El Matador and two beaches to the north into what is now an area known as Robert Meyer Memorial State Beaches. Since then, the area has become heavily patrolled and tickets are issued. The 1/4 mile stretch that is El Matador is the first closest beach out of the Los Angeles area and more or less enjoys its natural state.

> *DIRECTIONS:* From Los Angeles drive north on Highway 1 past Zuma Beach, in Malibu, to Trancas Canyon Road. Look for beach parking, about a mile north of the Trancas traffic signal. Park and take the trail down the cliff and go down the wooden steps made of old railroad ties.

GAVIOTA STATE BEACH
(NEAR LOS CRUCES, CA)

Our Last Report: The naked beach at Gaviota is found along the base of the bluffs just south of the main beach. Park your car at the FIRST pull-out south of the refinery, cross the freeway, and get back on the southbound lane for a hundred yards or so. The parking is only a stone's throw from Highway 101 so, keep your clothes on for a few more minutes!! Walk along the trail, cross the railroad tracks and you end up at the very edge of the bluffs overlooking the wide expanse of the Pacific Ocean. Head left along the bluffs until you come to a trail leading down to the beach below. There are lots of rocks to negotiate at the base, but a few yards south of the trail you'll find a small, intimate beach, with lots of friendly locals and a few visitors. The area is fairly well secluded and gawkers will have to be pretty dedicated to getting a view of the bare boys' butts from the cliffs.

But they can be seen. And like most California beaches, the naked area is defined by headlands at both ends of the beach. One note of caution, this part of the coast has both natural and man made oil leaks, leaving tar on the beach. Unless you want a big black splotch on your butt, be sure to always sit on your towel. If you DO get the muck on you, just use some oil-based skin lotion to rub it out. On an average day at this serene little beach, you'll see sea lions, seals, porpoise and occasionally a whale or two. The rocks also serve as attachments for kelp so you'll see lots of other, smaller forms of marine life there. (If you're REALLY lucky you may even see a Marine!) And, since this is primarily a gay beach, you'll also see plenty of your brothers experiencing the coast the way it ought to be experienced-Au Natural!

MORE MESA — AKA BATES BEACH
(NEAR SANTA BARBARA, CA)

Just north of Santa Barbara on Highway 101, this is the most popular nude beach south of Santa Cruz. The open expanse of its shoreline combines sweeping views with a wide ribbon of sand. Similar in size and feel, there is a festival-like atmosphere and real sense of community as that found at Black's Beach and Red Rock. In addition to nude jugglers, musicians, and even horseback riders who come in from the trails, you will find nude surfers and nude body surfers not generally seen elsewhere. Other activities include Frisbee, volleyball, and jogging. About a mile up shore is the northern-most end, which is isolated and gay.

DIRECTIONS: Like Black's Beach, there is a wooden stairway that helps you make your way down the cliff. Just take the Turnpike Rd. Exit south to Hollister Ave. Turn left, then take a right on Puente Dr., which becomes Vieja Dr. Look for parking when you see Mockingbird Lane. On the left Mockingbird is closed to traffic, so try to find a parking spot on Vieja instead. Walk down Mockingbird to the stairs that start near the eucalyptus grove. The path down the cliff is steep but easy. Gay men hang out on the northern tip of the long white sand beach. Bring sneakers or Aquasocks for the rough trail down.

OH MY GOD! HOT WELL
(NEAR PALM SPRINGS, CA)

This used to be a hot spring location, but the water has since dried up. Even without a place to soak, it has remained a popular nude sunbathing venue. Reports say it can be very cruisy, though both straight and gay nudists frequent this area.

DIRECTIONS: From CA86 in Salton City, turn west on CR-S22 (Borrego Salton Seaway) and go 2.8 miles. Turn left on the dirt road and go about a mile to the camping area.

PIRATE'S COVE — AKA AVILA BEACH
(NEAR SAN LUIS OBISPO, CA)

This part of California's shoreline is populated by seals and sea lions who like to sun themselves on rocks just off shore. Volleyball games can also be found on this 1/2 mile stretch of sand which runs parallel to 100 feet of a walled-in cliff. A private yet well-known beach, police tend to patrol the cliffs, hassling cliff-side voyeurs, while pretty much leaving the nudists to themselves. What a concept!

> *DIRECTIONS:* Take the Avila Beach Exit from Highway 101 and head west for 2 miles on Avila Rd. Look for a golf course on the right and a bluff and large oil sto rage tanks on top of a hill. Turn left onto Cave Landing Rd. and climb the hill for about 1/4 mile to the dirt parking lot. The straight nude beach is to your left. The gay section, which is small and very picturesque, is a little difficult to find. From the parking lot, follow the path toward the straight section and then look for a smaller path to the right, going down hill toward the cliff. At the end, you'll find a rope that dangles over the edge of a steep, rocky face about 30 feet above the beach. Use the rope to climb down and back up again. Not for the out of shape but worth the effort to get there.

Our Last Report: Near the quaint seaside village of Avila is another beautiful nude beach called Pirate's Cove. Take the Avila Beach exit from the 101 (just south of San Luis Obispo) and head in for about 2 miles. You'll pass a golf course on your right and then you'll see some storage tanks at the top of the hill on your left. Take Cave Landing Road up toward those tanks and over the hill. You'll arrive at a dirt parking lot overlooking a small cove to the left, leading to Shell Beach, and a somewhat protected set of rocks on the right. The cove to the left is the family beach, the rocky area to the right is the gay section. We recommend spending some time at the family beach. Gay men do congregate at the far end and this is a real beach with acres of sand and great access into the water. The walk down to the beach is simple, the people are friendly and the water is clean. Due to the unusual water temperature, I was able to swim on the last day of September. This far north that is unheard of! This is not part of the state beach system but nudity here is a well accepted custom at Pirate's Cove. You'll experience lots of sunshine, beautiful water and its remoteness precludes most gawkers.

The "gay" section of the beach is on the right of the parking lot. You have to REALLY want to get there, too. No handicap access!! Follow the trail through the bushes on the right of the parking lot. You will eventually end up at a point 15 feet or so above the beach. Now, grab the rope that is attached to the stump at your foot, and slowly lower yourself down the remaining portion. The beach here is really wonderland. Naked men can be found in all sorts of interesting little caves, alcoves and between rocks. The truly adventuresome can continue north, scampering over small headwalls to find other little coves, equally populated by naked men. If you're interested in wide beaches with easy ocean access, stay at the family side. But, over here, at the gay section, you can swim among the rocks if you are careful. On a sunny day, you can't go wrong at this intimate, picturesque beach!

SAN ONOFRE BEACH STATE PARK (NEAR SAN CLEMENTE)

One of the largest nude beaches in the State, San Onofre is State Beach sits next to Camp Pendelton Marine Base and in the shadow of twin nuclear reactors, which loom in the distance. This beach is special because o f its topography. Years of rainfall have left carved out areas from the rocky dunes. Many are naturally private areas.

Yoga is big here and many come here to find the tranquility offered by the dunes. During the summer it can get very busy. Police look for public sex but bother with little else. In addition to swimming, the usual can be found including sunbathing, volleyball, jogging, and playing Frisbee and paddleball.

> *DIRECTIONS:* Take the Basilone Rd. Exit from I-5 and head towards the nuclear power plant. Continue south to the park entrance (fee) and park at Trail Head No. 6. The nude beach is to the south - towards Camp Pendleton. Make sure you stay off military land. They do patrol. On occasion there have been reports of naked Marine sightings. From the parking area, find a carved out grove in the sand dunes that separate the beach. The descent is a cliff so this beach is not suited for those who are not physically able.

SILVER STRAND STATE BEACH (NEAR SAN DIEGO, CA)

This beach runs over 2 miles on a narrow strip of land between the ocean and San Diego Bay. Little silver shells are constantly washed up on shore in this area and cover the sand; hence the name. Fishing happily co-exists with surfing and swimming.

Nudity is popular on the north end near the Navy Reserve. The beach has picnic areas, restrooms, and lifeguards, along with camping for self-contained RVs and trailer campers.

> *DIRECTIONS:* From San Diego, take I-5 south to Highway 75 south at Coronado. Pass Silver Strand State Beach to Imperial City. At the first stoplight, take a right onto Rainbow Dr., then right onto Palm St. and go down to the end. No parking lot, so park on the street. Walk about 1 mile north along the beach, past the navel communications station. The beach is on city property and is patrolled periodically, so keep wraps handy.

COLORADO

NUDE CLUBS / GROUPS / ORGANIZATIONS

BOYS B BOYS (BBB)

Denver, CO
Contact: Tedd (303) 860-8407
Email: BoysBBoys@aol.com
Website: www.boysbeboys.com

A social nudist group for men ages 18-50.
Approx. 95 members
No dues or newsletter
Unlimited attendance
Potential members welcome
Events include monthly parties, potluck/dinners, pool/hot tub, theme/holiday, and hiking.

DENVER AREA NUDE DUDES (DAN-DS)

PO Box 300193
Denver, CO 80203-0193
Contact: Don J (303) 777-5036
Email: dands92@hotmail.com
        Dands9292@yahoo.com
Website: www.dan-ds.com/

Approx 90 members
Public newsletter
Yearly dues: $25 single / $50 couple
Limited attendance for house parties
Potential members
2 parties per month (fee)
Events include: indoor, potluck, theme/holiday, hot springs, mud baths, and swimming.

CLOTHING-OPTIONAL ACCOMMODATIONS

THE BUNK HOUSE LODGE

13203 Highway 9
Breckenridge CO 80424
(970) 453-6475
Email: info@bunkhouselodge.com
Website: www.bunkhouselodge.com

Year-round mountain retreat for gay men. 7 rooms with shared baths. Nudity permitted on the sundeck with hot tub. Sauna and video room. Breakfast included. Near skiing. 5 private double rooms, 1 dorm with 4 bunks, a BYOB bar, non-smoking facility (smoking permitted in bar only). We are the only GAY Lodge in the Colorado Mountains.

NUDE BEACHES / RECREATION AREAS

CONUNDRUM HOT SPRINGS (NEAR ASPEN)

This is a LONG hike (some do it in more than one day; camping overnight). Extremely remote with a well-established tradition of nude use, but worth the trip! Take plenty of food and water and be sure to check with the ranger station in Aspen for trail conditions before beginning your hike.

DIRECTIONS: From CO-82 go south on FS-102 (Castle Creek Road) four and a half miles. Turn right on FS-128 (rough road, 4-wheel drive vehicle recommended). Go one and a half miles and park near trail entrance (Trail 1981). Hike the trail for eight miles along the Conundrum Creek.

DREAM CANYON — AKA BOULDER CANYON (NEAR BOULDER, CO)

Very remote area that is traditionally a nude sunbathing spot. Most popular on summer weekends when those in-shape gay men make the hike to lie out naked on the flat rocks.

DIRECTIONS: From Boulder go west on Canyon Dr. a few miles. After the first tunnel, take the first right on Sugarloaf Rd. Just after mile marker 3, turn left on gravel road and keep to the left when you reach the fork. Follow down to parking area at trail head. Nude area is in bottom of canyon and requires good shoes to hike. Not for the faint of heart or out of shape.

CONNECTICUT

NUDE CLUBS / GROUPS / ORGANIZATIONS

BARE & GAY OF CONNECTICUT (B&G)

PO Box 380264
East Hartford, CT 06138
Email: bareandgay@yahoo.com - nudeclubct@aol.com
Website: www.bandgofct.org

Approx. 140 members
Members-only newsletter
Yearly dues: New members: $25 single / $30 couple
Renewals: $20 single / $30 couple
Limited attendance per host
Potential members welcome
1 party per month (fee)
Events Include: indoor/outdoor pool/hot tub, theme/holiday, annual Rapscallion dinner/dance.

SOUTHEASTERN CONNECTICUT BARE BODS (SCTBB)

281D6 Gardner Ave
New London, Ct 06320
(860) 440-3710
Email: SCtBB@hotmail.com

Approx. 70 members from 5 states (CT, RI, MA, NY & NJ) ranging in age from 30s to 70s with almost half the membership under 50. No membership dues, but a confidential screening is required to become a member. Socials are held each month on the second Saturday. A buffet, soft drinks, and snacks are provided. Guests are welcome at the monthly socials when accompanied by a member. Reservations are required for a social and must be made no later than 2 days before.

DELAWARE

NUDE CLUBS / GROUPS / ORGANIZATIONS

Sorry, None that we know of!

CLOTHING-OPTIONAL ACCOMMODATIONS

Sorry, None that we know of!

NUDE BEACHES / RECREATION AREAS

Sorry, None that we know of!

DISTRICT OF COLUMBIA

NUDE CLUBS / GROUPS / ORGANIZATIONS

LAMBDA SOLEIL

PO Box 1526
Rockville, MD 20849
Contact: (202) 466-1601
Email: tomnrick@aol.com
Website: www.lambdasoleil.org

Members only newsletter
Yearly dues
1- 3 events per month (fee)
Limited attendance

RENUDEPRIDE

Contact: Stephen G
Email: renudepride@yahoo.com

Monthly On-Line newsletter for members

NUDE BEACHES / RECREATION AREAS

P STREET BEACH IN ROCK CREEK NATIONAL PARK (WEST OF CONNECTICUT AVE., WASHINGTON, DC)

This is an "at your own risk" area. There are trails along the Rock Creek and wooded areas that are notorious for cruising. The "beach" is an open field that is often used by gay men for nude sunbathing. Be aware that this is exclusively at your own risk.

DIRECTIONS: From downtown DC, take the Rock Creek and Potomac Parkway north to Beach Drive. Exit onto Beach Drive, north, and take it to Broad Branch Road, make a left and then a right onto Glover Road, follow the signs to the Nature Center.

PUBLIC TRANSPORTATION: Take the red Metroline to the Friendship Heights Metro stop, transfer to the E2 bus line towards Fort Totten and get off at to Glover and Military Roads. Walk south on the trail up the hill to the Nature Center. Or take the red or green Metroline to the Fort Totten Metro stop, transfer to the E2 bus line towards the Friendship Heights and get off at Glover and Military Roads.

FLORIDA

NUDE CLUBS / GROUPS / ORGANIZATIONS

BEAR NAKED OF SOUTH FLORIDA (BNSF)

2300 Prarie Ave
Miami Beach, Fl 33140
305-672-2080
Email: Frank@castlepalms.com - info@bearnakedsouthflorida.org
Website: www.bearnakedsouthflordia.org

CENTRAL FLORIDA NATURISTS (CFN)

PO Box 677009
Orlando, FL 32867-7009
Website: www.central-fla-naturists.org

FORT LAUDERDALE GAY MEN'S NUDE SWIM CLUB

PO Box 4901
Fort Lauderdale, FL 33338
Email: GayNudeFla@aol.com

GAY NATURIST ORLANDO MALES EVOLVING SOCIALLY (GNOMES)

PO Box 692521
Orlando, FL 32869-2521
(407) 540-9391
Fax: (407) 540-9391
Email: gnomes@naturalmales.org
Website: www.naturalmales.org/gnomes

GOLD COAST BARE SKINS (GCBS)

PO Box 5072
Fort Lauderdale, FL 33310-5072
Email: membership@goldcoastbareskins.org
Website: www.goldcoastbareskins.org

JACKSONVILLE AREA NATURIST GROUP (JANG)

7126 Railey Cir
Jacksonville, FL 32210
(904) 777-4435
Email: jangnjax2@aol.com

Approx. 35 members (All Age Groups)
Members only newsletter
Unlimited attendance Annual dues
Monthly Parties, 3rd Saturday of the Month (No Fee)
Naked Men in the area are always welcome.

SOUTH FLORIDA MEN ENJOYING NATURE (SFMEN)

PO Box 970243
Coconut Creek, FL 33097-0243
Email: sfmen@naturalmales.org
Website: www.sfmenclub.com

SOUTHERN EXPOSURE (SE)

PO Box 8092
Tampa, FL 33674-8092
Contact: Ted (813) 237-2436
Email: southernexposure@naturalmales.org
Website: www.naturalmales.org/southernexposure

Approx. 70 members
Members-only newsletter
Yearly dues: $25 single / $40 couple
Potential new members welcome
2 parties per month – limited attendance (fee)
Events include: indoor/outdoor, potluck, pool/hot tub, movie night, theme/holiday, river/beach, card/game nights.

TAMIAMI AREA NUDISTS (TAN)

PO Box 60143
Fort Myers, FL 33906
(239) 945-7063
Email: Tamiamiareanude@aol.com
(Restricted to Netpass members only – free service)

TAMPA BAY NATURISTS (TBN)

PO Box 23051
Tampa, FL 33623-3051
Contact: (813) 961-3684
Email: tbn@tampabay.rr.com
Website: www.tampabaynaturists.org

Approx 95 members
Public newsletter
Yearly dues
Unlimited attendance
Potential members welcome
7-9 parties per month (fee)
Events include: indoor/outdoor, non-sexual video nights, sailing

WILDFYRE SOCIETY (WFS)

PO Box 8109
Fort Lauderdale, FL 33310-8105
(561) 276-6499
Email: WildFyreSociety@hotmail.com
Website: www.wildfyresociety.org

Miami/Fort Lauderdale/Palm Beach area
Approx. 1,000 members, plus 600 non-member contacts
E-newsletter, announcements, and invitations (except for members-only events)
go to entire Email list.
Yearly dues: $15
New memberships by referral of current members
3-4 events per month; unlimited attendance; modest fee.
Nude events include skating, square dancing, pool/beach parties, boating/
snorkeling/camping trips, shopping/theater/museum outings, holiday dinners.
Most events are open to non-members; parties at private homes are for members
only.

CLOTHING-OPTIONAL ACCOMMODATIONS

ATLANTIC SHORES RESORT

510 South St.
Key West, FL 33040
(888) 324-2996
(305) 296-2491
Email: atlshores@aol.com

Resort with mixed (gay/straight) clientele. Nudity permitted at the pool and on the sunbathing pier. 72 rooms and suites. Restaurant on premises. Welcome pets.

THE BAMBOO RESORT

2733 Middle River Dr
Fort Lauderdale FL 33306
(800) 479-1767
(954) 565-7775
Email: info@thebambooresort.com
Website: www.thebambooresort.com

Clothing-optional resort for gay men. 4 rooms with private baths, 1 studio apartment. Rooms have color TVs and VCRs (with complimentary video library). Secluded courtyard with heated pool, barbecue and sundeck. Continental breakfast included.

BIG RUBY'S KEY WEST

409 Applerouth Lane
Key West, FL 33040-6554
(800) 477-RUBY
(305) 296-2323
Fax: (305) 296-0281
Email: keywest@bigrubys.com
Website: www.bigrubys.com

A guesthouse for gay men with gay women welcome. Nude sunbathing and swimming permitted. 17 rooms, 14 with private baths. Lagoon-like swimming pool.

THE BLUE DOLPHIN INN

725 N. Birch Rd.
Fort Lauderdale, FL 33304-4024
(800) 893-BLUE
(954) 565-8437
Fax: (954) 565-6015
Email: dolphinftlaud@aol.com
Website: www.bluedolphinhotel.com

A superior Fort Lauderdale beach resort. Nudity permitted inside only. An intimate hotel with European flair for men.

THE BOHEMIA

825 Michigan Ave.
Miami Beach, FL 33139
(888) 883-4565
(305) 534-1322
Email: bohemiahouse@aol.com

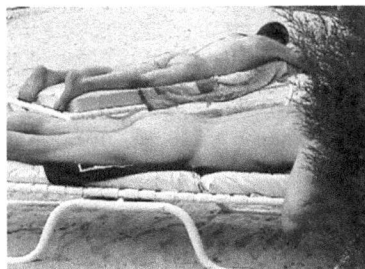

Apartments and rooms for men only. Non-smoking. Clothing-optional in hot tub and outdoor shower area. 6 blocks from the beach. Close to bars and restaurants. Extended continental breakfast included.

BRIGADOON II - BLU Q

Key West, FL
(305) 923-7245
Email: Captainstevekw@msn.com
Website: www.captainstevekw.com

Sailing charters on a luxury sailing yacht in Key West. All gay and clothing optional. Two- and five hour cruises available.

CAMP DAVID

2000 South Bishop's Point Road
Inverness, FL 34450
(352) 344-3445
Fax: (352) 344-3445
Email: campdavidfl@aol.com
Website: www.campdavidflorida.com

Camp Davis is a private membership, RV and Tent Retreat for men only. The entire 16 acres is clothing optional. They are dedicated to creating a quiet and peaceful atmosphere for the comfort of all their members. The management strives to maintain enjoyable surroundings; committed to a high level of cleanliness, organization, and customer service that is unsurpassed by any campground of its kind. The camp is secluded, remote, and characteristic of the landscape of central Florida. The property is heavily wooded, and includes three small lakes, a pool and patio area, hot tub, Rec. hall, bath house, trails and video lounge. 25 RV and tent campsites, 4 two person rooms in bunkhouse, 1 park model rental trailer accommodates up to 4 persons. Day passes available. No restrictions on nudity.

CHELSEA HOUSE BED AND BREAKFAST

709 Truman Ave
Key West FL 33040
(800) 845-8859
(305) 296-2211
Email: info@chelseahousekw.com
Website: www.chelseahousekw.com

Quaint resort in the heart of Key West. Clothing-optional sundeck. 16 rooms with private baths. Heated pool. Breakfast included.

COCONUT GROVE GUESTHOUSE

815 Fleming St
Key West FL 33040
(800) 262-6055
(305) 296-5107
Fax: (305) 296-1584
Email: info@coconutgrovekeywest.com
Website: www.coconutgrovekeywest.com

Bed and breakfast for gay men. Nudity permitted on sundeck and in swimming pool. 15 rooms; 13 with baths.

CORAL REEF GUESTHOUSE

2609 NE 13th Court
Fort Lauderdale, FL 33304
(888) ENJOY-IT (365-6948)
(954) 568-0292
Email: info@CoralReefGuesthouse.com
Website: www.coralreefguesthouse.com

"Award of Excellence" and "Best Location" Clothing optional Key West style guesthouse is upscale with, immaculately clean rooms ranging from 3 Standard, 2 Deluxe, 5 Studio to 1 Elite Suite (all with private bath). The tropical gardens with a spectacular heated pool and 14 man Jacuzzi amidst lush private surroundings. Complimentary continental breakfast, happy hour beverages, video library, Guest internet PC & wireless connection. Near Haulover State Park – Clothing Optional.

FLORIDA

ELYSIUM RESORT

552 North Birch Rd.
Fort Lauderdale, FL 33304
(800) 533-4744
(954) 564-9601
Fax: (954) 564-5618
Email: reservations@Elysiumresort.net
Website: www.ElysiumResort.net

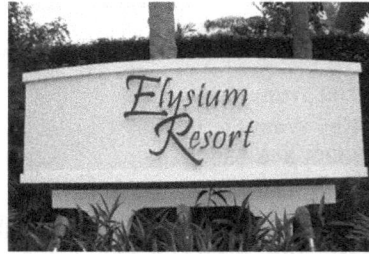

Private sundeck, 180 yards to the beach, video library, guest lounge, heated pool, internet and Email access, oversized and secluded Jacuzzi, Clothing Optional sundeck, gym and private baths.

EQUATOR RESORT

818 Fleming St
Key West FL 33040
(800) 278-4552
(305) 294-7775
Fax: (305) 296-5765
Email: equatr1@aol.com
Website: www.equatorresort.com

Key West's clothing-optional, all male resort. Hot tub, heated black pool, mix of 12 rooms and suites, all with private baths. Full American breakfast and evening cocktails daily. Three blocks from Duval St. nightlife.

EUROPEAN GUESTHOUSE

721 Michigan Ave.
Miami Beach FL 33139
(305) 673-6665
Fax: (786) 276-1911
Email: info@europeanguesthouse.com
Website: www.europeanguesthouse.com

Bed and breakfast for gay men and women. Nudity permitted on deck, Jacuzzi, and in garden area. 13 rooms 9 with private baths. Spa. Breakfast buffet included.

FLAMINGO INN

2727 Terramar Street
Fort Lauderdale, FL 33304
(800) 283-4786
(954) 561-4658
Fax: (954) 568-2688
Email: comments@theflamingoresort.com
Website: www.theflamingoresort.com

4 studios, 2 hotel rooms, 6 suites (all with private baths). Pool, workout room. Nudity permitted poolside.

HERON HOUSE COURT

412 Frances St
Key West FL 33040
(800) 932-9119
(305) 296-4719
Fax: (305) 296-1994
Email: info@heronhousecourt.com
Website: www.heronhousecourt.com

A gay guesthouse for men. Nude pool area for sunbathing. Continental breakfast. All rooms furnished with air conditioning, TV and refrigerator. Includes turndown service nightly during high season and holidays.

THE GUESTHOUSE

5100 La Croix Avenue
Orlando, FL 32812
(407) 857-4342
Email: lance407@aol.com

A laid back, quiet home setting, guesthouse for gay men. Nudity permitted anywhere. 2 rooms, pool. Continental breakfast included. 10 min from the Orlando Airport. Approx. 30 min to all attractions. A quiet place to unwind and relax by the pool and in the sun.

INN LEATHER GUEST HOUSE

610 SE 19th Street # 4
Ft Lauderdale FL 33316
(877) 532-7729
(954) 467-1444
Email: InnLeather610@aol.com
Website: www.innleather.com

Inn Leather was designed by Leathermen for Leathermen. We have proudly hosted the International Leather & Levi Community since 1999. We invite you to stay in our clothing-optional, all male compound and discover why we are your best option when staying and playing in Fort "Leatherdale"!

ISLAND HOUSE FOR MEN

1129 Fleming St
Key West FL 33040
(800) 890-6284
(305) 294-6284
Fax: (305) 292-0051
Email: IHKeyWest@aol.com
Website: www.islandhousekeywest.com

Key West's largest gay men's guesthouse. Newly renovated. Private clothing-optional compound with heated swimming pool. Poolside café and bar. Gym with machines, free weights, and aerobic equipment. Sauna, steam room, indoor and outdoor Jacuzzis, erotic video room. Clothing optional everywhere except the gym, where shoes and shorts are required.

MANGROVE VILLAS

1100 N Victoria Park Rd
Fort Lauderdale FL 33304
(800) 238-3538
(954) 527-5250

Resort for gay men by gay men. Private, fully equipped villas. Kitchens, large pool, Satellite TV, private baths. Nudity permitted poolside. 3 villas, 2 apartments, one studio.

MILL HOUSE INN

9603 Lillian Highway
Pensacola, FL 32506
(888) 999-4575
(850) 455-3400
Fax: (850) 458-6397

A bed and breakfast for gay men. 3 rooms with private baths. Nudity permitted in hot tub, in house, and on upper deck. Breakfast included.

MYSTIC LAKE MANOR

2398 W U.S. 90
Rte. 3, Box 2324
Madison, FL 32340
(850) 973-8435
Email: mysticlakemanor@aol.com
Website: www.mysticlakemanor.com

Castle with 3 private rooms with private baths, 3 private rooms with shared baths, and the "armory," which is a dorm-style room with 4 queen size beds. Pool and Jacuzzi inside property. Nudity permitted throughout. Full breakfast included.

NEW ZEALAND HOUSE

908 NE 15th Ave
Fort Lauderdale FL 33304
(888) 234-KIWI (5494)
(954) 523-7829
Fax: (954) 523-7051
Email: imakiwi@newzealandhouse.com
Website: www.newzealandhouse.com

All-male guesthouse. No restrictions on nudity. Heated pool. 8 deluxe rooms and private baths, Handicap accessible.

OASIS RESORT

823 Fleming St
Key West FL 33040
(800) 362-7477
(305) 296-2131
Fax: (305) 296-9171
Email: Oasisct@aol.com
Website: www.keywest-allmale.com

Guesthouse for gay men. 31 rooms (all with private bath). Two swimming pools, 24 hr. spa and sundeck. Complimentary expanded continental breakfast buffet and sunset wine and hors d'oeuvres. Nudity permitted poolside, sundeck, and Jacuzzi.

ORTON TERRACE

606 Orton Ave
Fort Lauderdale, FL 33304
(800) 323-1142
Fax: (954) 564-8646
Email: info@ortonterrace.com
Website: www.ortonterrace.com

Short walk to the Sebastian Street Gay Beach, or lounge in tropical clothing optional courtyard. Heated pool area provides plenty of warm Florida sunshine for that allover tan. Large and spacious Guest Rooms, extra large 1 Bedroom and Bedroom Apartments that all come equipped with a color TV, VCR, phone and stereo.

PILOT HOUSE GUESTHOUSE

414 Simonton St
Key West FL 33040
(800) 648-3780
(305) 293-6600
Website: www.pilothousekeywest.com

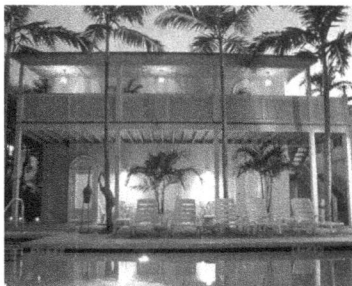

Pool and spa area. Nudity permitted in pool and spa. 14 rooms (all with private baths). Rooms are in Victorian house or poolside cabanas. Jacuzzis and hot tubs in cabanas. All welcome.

PINEAPPLE POINT

315 NE 16th Terrace
Fort Lauderdale, FL 33301
(954) 527-0094
Fax: (954) 527-0705
Email: info@pineapplepoint.com
Website: www.pineapplepoint.com

A gay guesthouse with mostly male clientele. 20 rooms, 5 suites (all with private baths). Heated pool and whirlpool. Nudity permitted in wet areas. Breakfast included. Near Haulover clothing optional beach. 10-man Jacuzzi. Complimentary champagne, 24 hours fitness center, massage studio, evening turn-down service. Daily pool-side happy hour. Complementary weekend barbeque. Free use of bicycles.

RICK'S BED & BREAKFAST

P.O. Box 22318
Orlando, FL 32830
(407) 396-7751
(407) 414-7751 (cell)
Email: rick@ricksbedandbreakfast.com
Website: www.ricksbedandbreakfast.com

A bed and breakfast for gay men. Nudity permitted anywhere, no restrictions. Pool. 2 rooms (one with private bath). Near Disney attractions. Breakfast included.

ROYAL PALMS RESORT

2901 Terramar St
Fort Lauderdale FL 33304-4012
(800) 237-7256 (PALM)
(954) 564-6444
Fax: (954) 564-6443
Email: info@royalpalms.com
Website: www.royalpalms.com

2003 Out & About "Editor's Choice" Winner. Deluxe accommodation. Private tropical gardens with clothing-optional pool, Jacuzzi and sundecks. 12 rooms (recently remodeled in 2000). Continental breakfast. Beer, wine, and soda also complimentary.

SAWMILL CAMPGROUND

21710 US 98
Dade City, FL 33523
(352) 583-0664
Fax: (352) 583-0896
Email: FLSawmill@aol.com
Website: www.flsawmill.com

150 RV and campsites, 3 cabins. Near Disney attractions. Nudity permitted in large pool area. Theme weekends.

THE SEA GRAPE HOUSE

1109 NE 16th Place
(at Old Dixie Highway)
Fort Lauderdale, FL 33305
(800) 447-3074
(954) 525-6586
Email: info@seagrape.com
Website: www.seagrape.com

Bed and breakfast for gay men. No restrictions on nudity. 7 rooms (2 with private bath). 2 pools, hot tub. Breakfast included. Close walk to Wilson Dr.

SEA ISLE RESORT

915 Windsor Lane
Key West FL 33040
(800) 995-4786
(305) 294-5188
Fax: (305) 296-7143

Resort exclusive for gay men. Nudity permitted in swimming pool and sundeck areas. 24 rooms, all with private baths. Swimming pool, nautilus gym, spa and private garden.

THE VILLAS

801 North Peninsula Drive
Daytona Beach, FL 32118
(386) 248-2020
Email: thevillabb@aol.com
Website: www.thevillabb.com

A bed and breakfast for all, catering to gay men. Others welcome. 6 rooms, pool, whirlpool. Nudity permitted in pool and sunbathing areas (advise manager first). Breakfast included.

VILLA VENICE

2900 Terramar St.
Fort Lauderdale, FL 33304
(877) 284-5522
(954) 564-7855
Email: info@villavenice.com
Website: www.villavenice.com

Resort with 23 guest rooms. Nudity permitted poolside.

NUDE BEACHES / RECREATION AREAS

APPOLLO BEACH
(CANAVERAL NATIONAL SEASHORE)

Unlike Playalinda, FL, there is no history of arrests and no anti-nudity law at Apollo Beach. The only problem is the limited parking and the next nearest parking lot is several miles away.

DIRECTIONS: Take the New Smyrna Beach/Highway 44 and exit off of I-95 going east. From the intersection of Highway 44 and A1A near New Smyrna Beach, go south for 8 miles and park in parking lot 5 or as far south as possible. Walk to the right, south of parking lot 5, to marker 29, where the nude area begins. Call (407) 867-2805 for beach information.

BOCA CHICA BEACH
(BIG COPPITT KEY, FL)

Key West locals and some guides refer to a naked beach on Boca Chica. Actually, this wonderful, secluded beach is on Big Coppitt Key, about 9 miles northeast of Key West. While nudity may not be legal, per se, the authorities tend to stay away form this remote area; but caution is advised. It is very rustic and delightful for walking. There are little patches of soft sand scattered throughout the path and lots of undergrowth and trees that offer some shade from the hot sun. This is very primitive so be sure to take your own "creature comforts" and lots of water.

DIRECTIONS: To get there from Key West, head northeast on US-1 about 9 miles from downtown. You'll see a Circle K convenience store on your right (south side of the road). Just after the store, turn right onto Old Boca Chica Road. You'll pass several trailer parks and some wilderness. When the road dead ends (about 5 miles) park and walk on the old road that follows the ocean. When you get to a Y in the road (about a half mile), you'll see several large boulders on the left. This is where the "naked beach" begins.

HAULOVER BEACH
(NORTH MIAMI BEACH, FL)

A popular nude beach in the Miami area for years.

> *DIRECTIONS:* Take Collins Ave. (A-1-A) north of Bal Harbour, through underpass. Straight and gay beach, gay area is the northern section. From NAKED Magazine Issue 5.01 By Joe Lonsway, Club Services Coordinator

If you're looking for a nude beach in Florida, good luck! Although Florida has an enormous coastline, with some of the best beaches in the United States (if not the world!), there are only two (yes TWO) beaches where nudity is legal – Apollo Beach near Cape Canaveral and Haulover Beach near Miami. Actually, Apollo Beach has had its share of problems and arrests lately, so I'm going to focus on Haulover Beach. Haulover Beach is located on Collins Avenue (A1A), between north Miami Beach and Hollywood (south of Fort Lauderdale). The beach is part of Haulover Park, a Miami-Dade County Park that includes a marina and a "textile" beach.

The north end of Haulover Beach is the clothing-optional area and the north part of THAT is the "gay" area. When you arrive, plan to park in the north lot to minimize your walk to the gay c/o section. The parking fee per car is reasonable. If you arrive late in the morning or early afternoon on a busy day, you might have to park in the south lot. While this is not traumatic, you will have to walk about one-half mile to the gay section.

After parking, I collected my chair, towel, sun tan lotion, small cooler and hat. This may sound like a lot to take to the beach but you should see all the "camping" gear some people bring. On one visit, I saw a couple with all the comforts of home, including champagne flutes!

Walking to the beach is part of the fun. After a stroll through the parking lot, you'll cross a Mangroves swamp on a picturesque boardwalk. You'll "cross" Collins Avenue by walking through the tunnel under the road and emerge by the restrooms and outdoor showers. Although this area is still "textile required," the day I visited I saw one brave man showering stark naked! No one seemed to mind as they went about their business.

As you approach the beach, there is a sign "warning" you that, "On the beach area beyond this point, you may encounter nude sunbathers." I sure hope so! A short walk across another boardwalk puts you right on the nude beach. On the right are a volleyball court (the unofficial game of nude beachgoers) and a concession stand that sells soft drinks, water, and sandwiches (the chicken is wonderful!) and they rent chairs. Also on the right is the predominately straight section while the gays tend to migrate to the left. While this is not a strict rule, it does seem to work out that way!

As I walked to the left, I saw a wide variety of people in various size groups. Some guys were by themselves while others were congregated in groups of up to eight.

The larger groups usually are veritable campsites complete with comfortable chairs, brightly colored umbrellas, large coolers and boom boxes spilling a variety of music from rap to opera! After finding a suitable location (right in the middle of some hunky, naked studs) I laid my towel out and stripped down. Suntan lotion is very important so I applied it liberally as some of my new neighbors watched.

I lay down on my towel with a short nap in mind-no easy task when literally hundreds of good looking men (and even a few good looking women!) wander up and down the beach. Oh well, I decided the nap could wait until later! I sat there and watched the parade. The naked beachgoers came in all shapes, sizes, colors and nationalities so there was plenty for everyone to enjoy.

It was a hot, sunny day (as it usually is on Haulover Beach) so I took a dip in the ocean. The water was a beautiful baby blue because the recent hurricanes and rains had churned it up a little; but it was still warm and soothing. I love walking on beaches and Haulover Beach is no exception. The entire nude section is about one-half mile long so there is plenty of opportunity to walk and see all your fellow nudists. Walking through the gay section is, of course, always fun, entertaining and even exhilarating. But don't miss out on all the wonderful people you can see and meet in the straight section, too! While there are a fair number of women there, don't forget that these same women also help attract a wide variety and large number of MEN—some of whom are quite attractive!

Lifeguard stations dot the landscape and are staffed by hunky, young men who keep an eye on the swimmers and beachgoers. The guards also (along with police beach patrol) keep an eye on everyone for general safety and to make sure there is no inappropriate behavior. Everyone seems pretty comfortable with couples (straight and gay) caressing a little, kissing, stroking each other's backs or stomachs, and frolicking in the foam. However, anything much more serious is definitely frowned upon.

Remember, sex in public is rude, illegal, and bad politics. That's what the opponents of social nudism like to focus on, so let's not give them any ammunition. When you find some hunky man on the beach whom you'd like to get to know, find a private location where you can explore each other more fully.

On any given weekend, Haulover Beach is host to nearly 15,000 people! It's is a great place to enjoy the south Florida sun, swim in the Atlantic Ocean and meet some nice locals and visitors.

PLAYALINDA BEACH
AKA CANAVERAL NATIONAL SEASHORE
(NEAR CAPE CANAVERAL, FL)

An attractive Central Florida beach with a designated section for naturists. The beach welcomes both straights and gays, but gay folks tend to gather in the northern section of the beach.

> *DIRECTIONS:* From I-95, take Exit # 80, at the 220 Mile Marker, and go EAST to Titusville, they call this Garden St. Go EAST to the end (the ocean). (While you are going EAST, you must cross over a draw bridge. IF you come to a fork in the road, fork right. If you come to a traffic light, continue EAST.) Once you get to the ocean, turn left, head North, to the end where you'll see Parking Lot # 13, at the Cul-de-Sac.

GEORGIA

NUDE CLUBS / GROUPS / ORGANIZATIONS

GREATER ATLANTA NATURIST GROUP (GANG)

PO Box 7546
Atlanta, GA 30357-0545
(404) 876-3064
Voicemail: (770) 351-5600
Email: gangatl-info@egroups.com
Membership: imen1@aol.com
Website: www.gangatl.org

RAINBOW NATURIST BROTHERHOOD (RNB)

PMB #287 463 Monroe Dr #102
Atlanta, GA 30308-1795
(678) 985-8890
* Second chapter is located in Athens, GA.
Email: info@rnbatlanta.org
Website: www.rnbofatlanta.blogspot.com

CLOTHING-OPTIONAL ACCOMMODATIONS

LYNWOOD PLACE BED & BREAKFAST

767 Lynwood St. SE
Atlanta, GA 30312
(404) 622-5622
Email: Lynwoodplace@aol.com

A bed and breakfast for gay men. Nudity permitted in all backyard areas including pool and hot tub. 3 rooms all with private bath. Breakfast included.

THE RIVER'S EDGE

2311 Pulliam Mill Rd
Dewy Rose GA 30634
(706) 213-8081
Fax (706) 213-6105
Email: dewy@camptheriversedge.com
Website: www.camptheriversedge.com

Private, membership-only clothing-optional campground and recreation area. Pool, showers, camping, 25 cabins, volleyball, hiking, fishing and more. 63 fun-filled acres of nude opportunity.

HAWAII

NUDE CLUBS / GROUPS / ORGANIZATIONS

MALES AU NATUREL OF HAWAII (MANOH)

PO Box 235426
Honolulu, HI 96823-3507
(808) 591-3826
Email: info@manoh.com
Website: www.manoh.com

Approx. 50 members
Yearly dues: $25 single / $35 couple
Potential members welcome
2 parties per month (fee)
Events include: indoor/outdoor, potluck/dinners, pool/hot tub, movie nights, theme/holiday, hiking, sailing/boating

PACIFIC MEN AT KALANI - OCEANSIDE RETREAT (PMK)

RR2, Box 4500
Pahoa Beach Road, HI 96778
(808) 965-7828
Email: richkoob@kalani.com
Website: www.kalani.com

Approx. 500+ members
Newsletter, Yearly dues
Potential members welcome
1 party a month
Events include: indoor/outdoor, potluck, pool/hot tub, theme/holiday, dance, exercise/aerobics, hiking, hot springs, kayaking, yoga, volleyball sports, week-long events

CLOTHING-OPTIONAL ACCOMMODATIONS

ABSOLUTE PARADISE BED & BREAKFAST

Pahoa, HI 96778
(888) 285-1540
(808) 965-1828
Located on Big Island of Hawaii
Email: info@absoluteparadise.tv
Website: www.absoluteparadise.tv

A gay and clothing-optional B&B just a short 5 minute walk to a clothing optional black sand beach. Close to natural hot ponds, steam caves, Lava Tree State Park, and Hawaii Volcanoes National Park. Ideally situated for some awesome snorkeling or hiking to secluded beaches and only a short drive to lush tropical botanical gardens and majestic waterfalls. All rooms have ocean views. In-ground pool and hot tub; tropical continental breakfast served daily.

THE BANANA PATCH

P.O. Box 1107
Kealakekua, HI 96750
(800) 988-2246
(808) 322-8888
Fax: (808) 322-7777
Email: info@bananabanana.com
Website: www.bananabanana.com

Private cottages – gay friendly. 1-bedroom cottage, 2-bedroom bungalow. Each unit is separate and private. On the Kona Coast of the Big Island. Each unit has Jacuzzi. No restrictions on nudity.

THE ALOHA GUEST HOUSE

84-4780 Mamalahoa Highway
Captain Cook, HI 96704
(800) 897-3188
(808) 328-8955
Email: vacation@alohaguesthouse.com
Website: www.alohaguesthouse.com

Bed and breakfast mostly for gay men. 4 rooms, one suite. Near Kona Coast beaches. Snorkel gear, mountain bikes, and boogie boards available. Nudity permitted outdoors for sunbathing. Breakfast included. Vacation rental, Kayak available.

HANA ACCOMMODATIONS

POB 564
Hana, Maui HI 96713
(800) 228-4262
(808) 248-7868
Email: info@hana-maui.com
Website: www.hana-maui.com

2 studios and 3 bedroom cottages with straight and gay clientele. Children allowed. Nude sunbathing allowed on sundeck only. Natural pool across street for nude sunbathing. Some units with ocean view.

KALANI OCEANSIDE RETREAT

RR 2 Box 4500
Pahoa-Beach Rd, HI 96778
(800) 800-6886
(808) 965-7828
Fax: (808) 965-0527
Email: kalani@kalani.com
Website: www.kalani.com

113 acre coastal resort with 67 rooms, straight and gay clientele, but men only for many gay events. Nudity permitted on the beach, at oceanfront, in pool, and evenings in the spa. Enjoy Hawaii's largest natural falls, crater lake, natural steam baths and thermal springs area, spectacular snorkeling, kayaking, and the world's most active volcano. Accommodations for every interest. "Tree House" units with king beds. "Cottages", "Ocean Vistas" and "Lodge" rooms – most with private bath. Full meal service (Breakfast, Lunch, Dinner); Olympic Pool/Spa; massage therapists, daily yoga, with many class and adventure options.

KALANIKAI BED & BREAKFAST

PO Box 1001
Kalaheo,HI 96741
(888)552-2777
(808) 332-5149

"Bathe in the Sun, Dance in the Warm Rain" Clothing optional retreat. Relax naturally at poolside or hot tub, in your Apt or suites, amongst landscape or on your lanai and anywhere in between.

MAHINA KAI

4933 Aliomanu Rd
Anahola Kauai HI 96703
(800) 337-1134
(808) 822-9451
Email: reservations@mahinakai.com
Website: www.mahinakai.com

Guesthouse for gay men and women. Clothing-optional but most nudity occurs around pool area and private patios off each room. 5 rooms with private baths, swimming pool and Spa. Daily continental breakfast.

MOHALA KE OLA

B&B RETREAT
5663 Ohelo Road
Kapaa, HI 96746
(888) GO-KAUAI (465-2824)
(808) 823-6398
Email: kauaibb@aloha.net
Website: www.waterfallbnb.com

Gay-friendly bed and breakfast. 3 rooms. Pool, hot tub, river nearby. Nudity permitted in pool and hot tub areas. Breakfast included.

NUDE BEACHES / RECREATION AREAS

DONKEY BEACH
(KAUAI, HI)

A crescent shaped beach popular with both straight and gay nudists on the east coast of Kauai. Lately there have been reports of ticketing (no arrests) due to stepped up enforcement. As with all beaches, proceed with caution. After all, nudity is illegal in Hawaii.

> *DIRECTIONS:* Take Route 56 north from Kapaa toward Anahola. Watch for a cane plantation road on the right between mile markers 11 and 12. Take the cane road and bear right. Donkey Beach will be ½ mile on the left.

HONOKAHAU HARBOR — AKA QUEEN'S BATH BEACH
(BIG ISLAND, HI)

Popular with both straights and gays, this is an attractive and often photographed beach. In 1999 the National Park Service placed a permanent ban on nudity on this beach. Because these "bans" tend to come and go, we are still listing this beach. Inquire locally about what's currently going on for nude sunbathers.

> *DIRECTIONS:* The beach is north of Kailua and south of the Kailua-Kona airport. Head toward the ocean on the Honokohau Harbor Rd. Bear right until the road deadends just past the Kona Marina.. Follow the main road around the marina. Look for a sign pointing to the beach and "NB" painted on the rocks. The beach has a gay section.

KEHENA BEACH
(BIG ISLAND, HI)

Black sand beach created by a volcanic eruption in 1955. Popular with both gay and straight nudists.

> *DIRECTIONS:* From Hilo, take HI-11 south about 8 miles to Keaau, then turn left on HI-130. Continue for approximately 20 miles to intersection with HI-137 at the coast (Kalapana is too far). Make a sharp left onto HI-137 and continue for approximately 4 more miles. Park near milepost 19. A trail near this mile marker takes you to the beach. Go left (northeast) on the beach to reach the nude section.

LITTLE MAKENA BEACH
(MAUI, HI)

A great beach located on sunny Maui. Good body surfing.

DIRECTIONS: The beach is located at the end of Route 31. Go a mile past the Maui Prince Hotel, turn right onto a rough road to the parking area. The nude beach is to the right of the lava flow.

LYDGATE BEACH
(KAUAI, HI)

Part of Lydgate Park. The south end of the beach is traditionally nude.

DIRECTIONS: Go north on HI-56 from Lihue. Just past Wailua Golf Course, turn right on Leho Drive. Proceed less than a quarter mile, then turn right onto Nehe Road. Park at the end of the road and walk to the beach. At restrooms, walk south (right as you're facing the water).

PAHOA STEAM VENTS
(BIG ISLAND, HI)

The steam from the sulfur fumes that create these vents is visible from the highway. Like a natural steam room, you'll need to bring plenty of water to drink and also to wash yourself off with. Can get very hot during the day, so morning or evening visits are the most comfortable.

DIRECTIONS: From Hilo, take HI-11 south approximately 8 miles to Keaau, then turn left on HI-130. Continue south for approximately 10 miles to Pahoa. Three miles past Pahoa park in the scenic overlook turnout near milepost 15. Take any one of the short trails from the parking area through the woods to the vents.

PUAKO BEACH
(BIG ISLAND, HI)

One of Hawaii's lesser-known nude beaches. This beach has a significant gay usage. Remember, nudity is illegal in Hawaii, so use caution before disrobing.

DIRECTIONS: Head north on HI 19 (Queen Kaahumanu Highway) from Kailua Kona. Turn left onto Puako Beach Drive (about 30 miles), then take the first right. Proceed to telephone pole number 67. Park near the pole. On the beach, walk to the north end for the nude section (right as you face the water).

SECRET BEACH
(KAUAI, HI)

A beautiful beach protected by a 300 foot cliff. Again, as with Donkey Beach, there have been recent reports of ticketing and private security officers asking bathers to cover up. This is due to a property developer who is building on the area above the cliffs. Use caution, nudity is not legal in Hawaii.

> *DIRECTIONS:* Take route 56 north/west from Kapa to Kilauea. Just after the 23 mile marker, turn sharply right at the Shell gas station. Go 100 feet and turn left onto Kilauea Rd. From the Shell station, go 1.35 miles to Kauapea Rd. on your left.

Use caution, nudity is not legal in Hawai.

ILLINOIS

NUDE CLUBS / GROUPS / ORGANIZATIONS

CHICAGO AREA NATURIST SONS (CANS)

3023 N Clark St #367
Chicago, IL 60657-5261
Email: cansguys@cansguys.org
Website: www.cansguys.org

Approx. 120 members
Members-only newsletter
Yearly dues: $20 single / $25 couple
Unlimited attendance
Potential members welcome
2 + 4 parties per month (fee)
Events include: dinners, bowling, camping, and recitals

WINDY CITY GAY NATURISTS (WCGN)

1538 Rosemont Ave. #1
Chicago, IL 60660-1323
Contact: Earl (312) 494-2654
Email: windycitygaynude@aol.com
Website: www.windycitygaynaturists.org

Approx. 110 members
Members-only newsletter
Yearly dues: $25 for singles, $40 for couples residing at same address. Renewals are $20 for singles and $30 for couples.
Potential members welcome
Guests may attend 3 events
Club hosts four to six events per month (fee)
Events include: indoor/outdoor swimming, massage, dinners, cocktail parties, bowling, theatre, holiday-theme parties

INDIANA

NUDE CLUBS / GROUPS / ORGANIZATIONS

BARE INDY BOYS (BIB)

PO Box 421
Brazil, IN 47834-0421

Approx. 50 members, Members-only newsletter, Yearly dues
Unlimited attendance, Potential members welcome
1-2 parties per month (fee)

IOWA

NUDE CLUBS / GROUPS / ORGANIZATIONS

GAY MEN ENJOYING NUDITY (G-MEN)

301 N 5th St
Eldridge, IA 52748-1124
(563) 285-4375

Approx. 95 members
Newsletter, No yearly dues, Unlimited attendance, Potential members welcome.
1-2 parties per month. Events include: Indoor/outdoor, potluck

CLOTHING-OPTIONAL ACCOMMODATIONS

RACCOON RIVER RESORT

2678 324th Way
Des Moines, IA
(515) 279-7312
(515) 996-2829

Resort for gay men and women located on the riverfront of the Raccoon River. Nature trails, 4 beaches, camp sites, bunk house, teepee (sleeps 8), and RV hookups. Hot tub, sauna and food available. Nudity permitted around lodge and in camping areas in the evening, during the day on the beaches and in camping areas. Nudity permitted in hot tub and sauna at all times.

NUDE BEACHES / RECREATION AREAS

GLENWOOD SANDPIT
(NEAR COUNCIL BLUFFS, IA)

This is an area where your discretion is highly recommended. As with many nude beaches, this has had hot and cold reports of citations, etc. This "pond" was formed when land was removed to build ramps for Interstate 29. There are a lot of cottonwood trees that shield the view from the road. The latest report said the sheriff's department had the biggest problem with people parking on both sides of the road (a traffic hazard). So...if you go, park on the same side of the road that you see all the other cars!

> *DIRECTIONS:* Take I-29 south approximately 12 miles from Council Bluffs. Exit Glenwood (Exit 35). Continue on gravel road on the west side of I-29 for about 2 miles and then turn left at the stop sign. Go another half mile and the sand pit is on the right. Walk to south and west sides of the pond.

KANSAS

NUDE BEACHES / RECREATION AREAS

LAKE EDUN
(TOPEKA, KS)

PO Box 1982
Email: Bornnude@aol.com
Website: www.lakeedun.com

This is a privately owned lake with clothing-optional status granted by the owner. A day-use fee is charged or annual membership is required. The best feature of this area is the cable that runs across the lake. Climb a 35-foot tower and ride the pulley out over the water to drop your naked self into the lake!

There is contact information for this facility:
Box 1982, Topeka, KS 66601
(785) 478-BARN (recorded message)
Email: enude@lakeedun.com.

DIRECTIONS: From I-470 southwest of Topeka, take Exit 4 and go south on Gage Boulevard approximately 2 miles. Turn right onto SW 53rd Street and go another 3 miles. Turn left onto Indian Hills Road and proceed about one quarter mile. Look for the first gate on the right side of the road. Park on the shoulder of the road or in the lot if the gate is open. Take the trail to the barn where you will pay your entrance fee.

KENTUCKY

NUDE CLUBS / GROUPS / ORGANIZATIONS

KENTUCKIANA GAY NUDISTS (KGN)

PO Box 201
Lexington, KY 40588-0201
(502) 226-4909
Email: kgn-president@gay.com
Website: www.getnaked.info
Contact: Donald G.

Potential members welcome.
Passion Tropical

LOUISIANA

NUDE CLUBS / GROUPS / ORGANIZATIONS

GAY ARK-LA-TEXANS INTO NUDITY (GAIN)

PO Box 291
Coushatta, LA 71019-0291
(318) 932-8700 (You will reach a live person after 6:00 PM CST.)
Email: GAINweblink@webtv.net

CLOTHING-OPTIONAL ACCOMMODATIONS

THE GREEN HOUSE INN

1212 Magazine Street
New Orleans, LA 70130
(800) 966-1303
(504) 525-1333
Fax: (504) 525-1383
Email: info@thegreenhouseinn.com
Website: www.thegreenhouseinn.com

Bed and breakfast with mostly male clientele. 7 rooms. Pool, oversized outdoor Jacuzzi, waterfall, tropical grounds. Nudity permitted in pool and Jacuzzi areas. Continental breakfast included. Off-street parking.

MACARTY PARK GUESTHOUSE

**3820 Burgundy Street
New Orleans, LA 70117-5708
(800) 521-2790
(504) 943-4994
Fax: (504) 943-4999
Email: macpar@aol.com**

Guesthouse mostly for gay men. 5 rooms, 1 suite, 2 cabins. Nudity permitted in hot tub and pool areas.

ROBER HOUSE

**820 Ursulines St.
New Orleans, LA 70116-2422
(504) 529-4663
Fax: (504) 529-1742
Email: stay@roberhouse.com
Website: www.roberhouse.com**

Condo rentals in the French Quarter, mostly for gay men. 5 apartments (all with private baths). Nude sunbathing permitted poolside (subject to objection by other guests).

ROYAL BARRACKS GUESTHOUSE

**717 Barracks Street
New Orleans, LA 70116
(888) 255-7269
(504) 529-7269
Fax: (504) 529-7298
Email: info@rbgh.com
Website: www.rbgh.com**

Guesthouse mostly for gay men located in the French quarter. 5 rooms, one suite. Nudity permitted in hot tub and courtyard.

NUDE BEACHES / RECREATION AREAS

COUNTRY CLUB

634 Louisa Street
New Orleans, LA 70117
Phone: (504) 945-0742

This facility is a unique place for gay recreation featuring a clothing-optional swimming pool, hot tub, and sundeck.

MAINE

NUDE CLUBS / GROUPS / ORGANIZATIONS

BARE BEARS OF MAINE (BBM)

PO Box 2277
South Portland, ME 04116-2277
(207) 799-1822
Email: barebearsmaine@yahoo.com
Website: www.barebears.com
New members welcome
Several parties each month ($2 fee)
Regular gatherings second Saturday of each month
Events include: indoor/outdoor, potluck, theme/holiday

CLOTHING-OPTIONAL ACCOMMODATIONS

MAPLE HILL FARM B&B INN

11 Inn Road
(off the Outlet Road)
Hallowell, ME 04347
(207) 622-2708
(800) 622-2708
Fax: (207) 622-0655
Email: stay@MapleBB.com
Website: www.MapleBB.com

Country Bed and Breakfast Inn with modern luxuries that is gay-friendly. 8 large double rooms, one suite (all with private bath). Nudity permitted in woods around secluded swimming hole on property and on private sundecks. Some rooms have private huge double whirlpool tubs, fireplaces, and private decks. Breakfast included. Common guest kitchenette with refrigerator and microwave. Full liquor service. 130 acres to explore and hundreds of acres of public land adjacent to farm property. Farm animal menagerie of pets.

MAINE

NUDE BEACHES / RECREATION AREAS

LAKE WOOD
(NEAR BAR HARBOR, ME)

Popular local swimming area where just about everyone is naked. Crowd is reported to be significantly gay. Sunning on granite ledges.

DIRECTIONS: Take Exit 45 from I-95 (near Bangor) and go east on I-395 to the end of the freeway. Connect with Alt US-1 and continue for approximately 25 miles to Ellsworth, where you will turn right onto ME-3. Continue another 10 miles to the coastal waters and cross onto Mount Desert Island. Stay on ME-3 for another 6 miles to Hulls Cove. Turn right onto Crooked Road (Acadian Restaurant is your landmark). Pass quarry operations after a half mile and turn left onto the second dirt road after the gravel pits. The road is marked by a sign that gives hours of public access to the park. Park in the first grassy parking area before the turn into the paved parking area. Take the trail that leads through the woods, then an open area, then woods again to the ledges. Smaller trails to the right lead to the nude area. This is about a 10-minute hike.

MARYLAND

NUDE CLUBS / GROUPS / ORGANIZATIONS

BALTIMORE AREA NUDE DUDES (BAND)

123 W Barre St #304
Baltimore, MD 21201
(410) 539-6435
Email: bandbaltimore@hotmail.com

MASSACHUSETTS

NUDE CLUBS / GROUPS / ORGANIZATIONS

BARE BOTTOMS / BOSTON (BB/B)

16 Allston St #3
Dorchester, MA 02124
(617) 436-9802
Email: barebottomsbos@webtv.net
Website: www.geocities.com/westhollywood/village/2626

BOSTON AREA NATURIST GROUP (BANG)

PO Box 180036
Boston, MA 02118-0001
(617) 783-3831
Email: bang@bangma.org
Website: www.bangma.org

Approx. 140 members
Members-only newsletter
Yearly dues
Potential members welcome
At least 1 party per month (fee)

NAKED YOGA FOR MEN

Cambridge, MA
Email: redhead_02319@yahoo.com
Website: http://groups.yahoo.com/group/naked_yoga_for_men

We meet twice weekly in a dance studio. Our instructor is a former Boston Ballet Co. Dancer. We are proud of the friendly, not-so-cruisy, atmosphere we have created and aim to keep it that way.

GREATER SPRINGFIELD GAY NUDISTS (GSGN)

1981 Memorial Dr PMB #146
Chicopee, MA 01020
(413) 783-2614
Emails: funwithwil@aol.com

120 members from all New England
Meets once a month
Any male 18+ is welcome

PILGRIM NATURISTS OF NEW ENGLAND (PILGRIM NATURISTS)

PO Box 320273
Boston MA 02132-0003
(866) 867-2932
Email: pilgrim@sunclad.com
Website: www.sunclad.com/pilgrim

WORCESTER AREA NAKED GUYS (WANG)

c/o FB 3222 Arbor Dr
Shrewsbury, MA 01545
(508) 842-8885
Email: gaynudistinmass@aol.com
Website: www.gaynudistinmass.tripod.com

MASSACHUSETTS

CLOTHING-OPTIONAL ACCOMMODATIONS

CARL'S GUESTHOUSE

68 Bradford St (Corner of Court St)
Provincetown MA 02657
(800) 348-CARL
(508) 487-1650
Email: infowp@carlsguesthouse.com
Website: www.carlsguesthouse.com

Very popular guesthouse for gay men, with clothing-optional sundeck and shower area. Excellent central location. 14 guest rooms with private baths and shared baths. 3 single person rooms (twin beds). 4 medium rooms for 1 or 2 persons (full beds). 7 larger rooms for 1 or 2 persons (Queen beds). Open year round. Off Season Discounts often available to individual members of adult gay groups. Also special rates for academic students between 18 and 30. Both daily and special weekly rates available. (Inquire at check-in time)

"…Where strangers become friends…" Carl's is clean, comfortable, affordable and friendly with an excellent central location.

FOUR GABLES

15 Race Road
Provincetown, MA 02657
(866) 487-2427
Email: info@fourgables.com
Website: www.fourgables.com

A cottage colony mostly for gay men. 2 apartments, 3 cottages. Nudity permitted in hot tub and on sundeck.

ROMEO'S HOLIDAY

97 Bradford Street
Provincetown, MA 02657
(877) MY-ROMEO (697-6636)
(866) PTOWNMEN
(508) 487-6636
Fax: (508) 487-3082
Email: info@romeosholiday.com
Website: www.romeosholiday.com

Guesthouse mostly for gay men. 8 rooms (4 with private baths). Nudity permitted in hot tub and on rear sundeck. Continental breakfast included.

SUNSET INN

142 Bradford Street
Provincetown, MA 02657
(800) 965-1801
(508) 487-9810
Fax: (508) 487-7820
Off-season phone: (954) 730-7287
Email: sunset1@capecod.net
Website: www.sunsetinnptown.com

Guesthouse mostly for gay men. 20 rooms (14 with private bath and A/C, 6 with shared baths on third floor). Nudity permitted on third floor sundeck. Continental breakfast and parking included.

NUDE BEACHES / RECREATION AREAS

GAY HEAD BEACH — AKA MOSHUP BEACH
(MARTHA'S VINEYARD, MA)

On the southwest extension of Martha's Vineyard, the multi-colored cliffs make this beach appear to be somewhere in the southwest rather than in New England. Nudity is common here (both gay and straight) and rangers do not bother nude bathers.

DIRECTIONS: This is accessible by ferry only. Ferries leave from New Bedford, Woods Hole, and Hyannis port. All ferries dock at Vineyard Haven on the north end of the island. Busses are available to Gay Head. If you rent transportation (car, moped, bicycle), take Old Country Road for about 6 miles. Turn right onto South Road and go another 12 miles (through Gay Head) then turn left onto Moshup Trail and look for parking for Moshup Beach. At beach, go right and walk about a quarter mile to boulders.

HERRING COVE
(NEAR PROVINCETOWN, MA)

Mostly gay beach, just outside of Provincetown.

DIRECTIONS: Take US-6 east along Cape Cod peninsula. When you reach Orleans, the freeway ends and is a regular highway that runs northward. Go 26 miles to Provincetown. Continue past Provincetown to where US-6 ends at Cape Cod Bay where you will see signs for Herring Cove. Also easily accessible from Boston.

TRURO BEACH
(TRURO, MA)

A popular nude beach on the Atlantic side of Truro (near the end of Cape Cod). This is national seashore land so, of course, nudity is illegal; but this beach is traditionally clothing-optional without too much hassle. The rule is simple: if you see a dune buggy coming, cover up! When it passes, get naked again!

DIRECTIONS: Take US-6 east along Cape Cod peninsula. When you reach Orleans, the freeway ends and is a regular highway that runs northward. Go 16 miles north of Orleans to Truro. Parking permits are available at the Truro Town Hall. Go east on Long Nook Road until you reach the ocean. The area traditionally known for nudity is between Ballston Beach (south) and Long Nook Beach (north).

WESTFIELD RIVER
(NEAR SPRINGFIELD AND NORTHAMPTON, MA)

Wide sandy beach and a pool in the river for swimming. Predominantly used by gay men with week days being almost exclusively gay. Latest report had problems listed with parking. Signs are posted saying cars parked over 30 minutes will be towed. There is no alternative parking in the area, so bicycling may be the best way to get here.

DIRECTIONS: Take Exit 18 off I-91 in Northampton. Follow signs for MA-9 west through Northampton. Continue for another 20 miles on MA-9 to Cummington. One mile past the town sign (on left side of road), park in large pull-off on the left side of the road. Walk down the bank and wade across the shallow water to the trail that goes into the woods. Total hike is about a half mile.

MICHIGAN

NUDE CLUBS / GROUPS / ORGANIZATIONS

NORTHERN EXPOSURE GREAT LAKES (NEXPO)

PO Box 68255
Grand Rapids, MI 49516-8255
(616) 776-0083
(616) 651-4494
Email: unofour@hotmail.com

Approx 50 members
Membership only newsletter
Yearly dues
Unlimited attendance
Some of the activities include potluck, cookouts, and dinners, campouts, trips and other fun things for all men. Guests and potential/members welcome. 1 party per month

NUDE BEACHES / RECREATION AREAS

OVAL BEACH CITY PARK
(NEAR SAUGATUCK, MI)

Very popular with gays. Located on Lake Michigan. Large area of dunes and trails known for cruising where nudity is generally tolerated. Nudity is not allowed right on the beach, but there is a lagoon where nude swimming is okay as long as you stay hidden from boaters. Check locally for the current enforcement climate.

DIRECTIONS: Take I-196 southwest to Saugatuck. Exit onto Washington Road and go right for approximately 1 mile. Bear left onto Old US-31 and continue to Douglas. About 1 mile past the lake, turn right onto Ferry Street, which will become Park Street. Go to Perryman and turn left (sign for Oval Beach). Dead end is parking lot. Nude area is on private property with entrance on the north end of the beach. An entrance fee of $3-$5 is collected (in addition to parking fee).

MINNESOTA

NUDE CLUBS / GROUPS / ORGANIZATIONS

MINNESOTA NATURISTS (MN INC)

PO Box 580811
Minneapolis MN 55458-0111
Email: mnnature@aol.com - info@mnnaturists.org
Website: www.mnnaturists.org

NAKED MINNESOTA (N-MINN)

PO Box 8614
Minneapolis, MN 55408-0614
Email: nakedmn@aol.com - questions@nakednm.org
Website: www.nakedmn.org

Approx. 175 members
Members-only newsletter
Yearly dues
Unlimited attendance
Potential members welcome
2-4 parties per month (fee)

NUDE BEACHES / RECREATION AREAS

LESTER RIVER FALLS
(DULUTH, MN)

Water is extremely cold! But this is a great place to sun your buns on the granite. Predominantly used by gay men.

DIRECTIONS: Take MN-61 northeast which will become London Road. Continue to 60th Avenue East and turn left. Go one block and turn right onto Superior Street. Go 2 blocks (cross bridge), then turn left onto Lester River Road after the Lester Park Golf Course sign. Go slightly over one mile from the intersection and look for a small parking area on the left side of the road.

PARK POINT BEACH
(DULUTH, MN)

This is the place for solitude. Very isolated (even though it's close to Duluth and Superior, WI).

DIRECTIONS: Go northeast on Superior Street. Turn right onto Lake Avenue (this intersection is near the convention center). Follow Lake Avenue over the Lift Bridge and continue until it ends at Minnesota Avenue. Veer left and continue on Minnesota Avenue to the end. Park in the Park Point Recreation Area. Walk across the dunes to the Lake Superior side of the narrow island and go to the right (when facing water). Walk until you see either seclusion or other nude bathers.

MISSOURI

NUDE CLUBS / GROUPS / ORGANIZATIONS

KANSAS CITY STRIP (KCS)

PO Box 28291
Gladstone, MO 64188-0291

Approx 115-125 members
Members-only newsletter
Yearly dues: $12 single/ $24 couple
Potential members welcome
2-3 parties per month
Events include: indoor, pool/hot tub, movie night, theme/holiday, morning coffees

RA OF SAINT LOUIS

PO Box 190086
Saint Louis, MO 63119-0086
Contact: Earle (314) 287-3787
Email: nuderamen@aol.com

Approx. 60+ members
Members-only newsletter
Yearly dues
Unlimited attendance
Potential members welcome
2 party per month (fee)

CLOTHING-OPTIONAL ACCOMMODATIONS

CACTUS CANYON CAMPGROUND

P.O. Box 266
Ava, MO 65608
(417) 683-9199
Email: mail@cactuscanyoncampground.com
Website:
www.cactuscanyoncampground.com

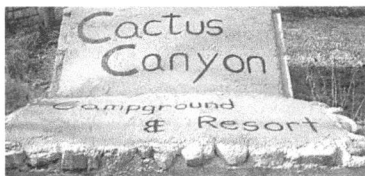

Campground mostly for gay men. One furnished room, 8-bed bunk house, 75 campsites, and 12 RV hook-ups. Hot showers, hot tub, and sauna. Campground is clothing-optional.

COUNTRY'S GETAWAY

119 Big Bend Lane
Steelville, MO 65565
(573) 775-5534
Email: countrysgetaway@yahoo.com

Campground for men only. 20 campsites, outdoor and indoor shower/toilet. Electrical hook-ups available. No restrictions on nudity.

ST. LOUIS GUESTHOUSE

1032 Allen Avenue
St. Louis, MO 63104
(314) 773-1016
Website: www.stlouisguesthouse.com

Nudity permitted in courtyard and hot tub areas. A guesthouse in historical Soulard between Busch Brewery and the Old Farmers Market with a 100% gay clientele. Five units with queen size beds, cable TV, VCR, AC, wetbar with refrigerator and microwave. Private bath in each room and private entrances. Nudity allowed at Hot-Tub. Two gay bars and restaurants next door. Non-smoking facility.

NUDE BEACHES / RECREATION AREAS

MEXICO GRAVEL LAKE — AKA WACO BEACH (COLUMBIA, MO)

A small lake traditionally used by gay men for nude bathing. Located near the 3M plant. Reports talk of a section with pieces of carpet that is known for nude bathing.

DIRECTIONS: Take Exit 128A from I-70 and go north on US-63 for 2 miles. Turn right onto CR-B (Paris Road) and go just under two miles. Turn right onto Waco Road immediately past the 3M plant. Go to the end of the road and park. A path leads to the small lake on the left. The pieces of carpet are near the southwest corner of the lake.

NEBRASKA

NUDE CLUBS / GROUPS / ORGANIZATIONS

LINOMA BARES (LOB)

PO Box 24547
Omaha, NE 68124
(402) 553-5944
Email: linomabares@yahoo.com

Approx. 95 members
Members-only newsletter
Yearly dues: $17 single / $25 couple
1-2 parties per month
Events include: potluck

NUDE BEACHES / RECREATION AREAS

TWO RIVERS STATE RECREATION AREA (NEAR OMAHA, NE)

The sandbars on the Platte River off the TRSRA property have been used by nudists. This is private property, but apparently whoever owns it does not hassle nude bathers. Park rangers are reported not to bother nude bathers off the TRSRA property.

DIRECTIONS: Take I-80 west from Omaha. Approximately one mile southwest of the junction of I-680 and I-80, take Exit 445 and go west on NE-92. Continue to Venice (very small community). Look for Q Street and turn left. If you cross the Platte River, you've gone too far. Follow the signs to Two Rivers State Recreation Area. After paying the entrance fee, take the first left after the entrance. Drive to the camping area where you should park. Follow the small dirt road south approximately one mile. A fence marks the TRSRA boundary. Hop the fence to the sandbars.

NEVADA

NUDE CLUBS / GROUPS / ORGANIZATIONS

GAY NATURISTS OF GREATER RENO (GNGR)

PMB 123
3495 Lakeside Dr
Reno, NV 89509-4841
(775) 825-6241 Bob
Gay Male Nudist club
Email: Digambara@gay.com

Approx. 15 members
Periodic newsletter
Meet Monthly
Sexual Policy: We explore courteously
Activities: House parties, nude hiking/camping/swimming/hot springs/videos and lots of travel. Located in the heart of the Sierra Nevada mountains.

LAS VEGAS SUNRUNNERS (LVS)

855 E Twain Ave. #123473
Las Vegas, NV 89109-0818
(702) 363-6862
Email: SunRunners@SunRunners.port5.com

Approx. 80 members
Members-only newsletter
Yearly dues: $10 single/couple
Potential members welcome
2 parties per month
Events include: indoors/outdoors, potluck, pool/hot tub, theme/holiday, hiking, hot springs, house-boating/canoeing

SIERRA TAHOE AREA NUDE DUDES (STAND)

5919 Simons Dr.
Reno, NV 89523
(775) 787-0890
Email: ntvtouch@aol.com - pauldcain@aol.com

CLOTHING-OPTIONAL ACCOMMODATIONS

BLUE MOON RESORT

2651 Westwood Drive
Las Vegas, Nevada 89109
(866) 789-9194
(702) 361-9099
Fax: (702) 361-9110
Email: info@bluemoonlv.com
Website: www.bluemoonlv.com

Jacuzzi Grotto with 10 ft cascading waterfalls. Rejuvenate in a 400 sq ft steam room, or lay out in lavishly landscaped clothing optional pool area complete with private cabanas. Fabulously designed Sundeck, and 10-man spa. Close to strip. 45 rooms and suites. Coffee house, media room with complementary high-speed internet access. Hotel transportation available.

CHAPMAN GUESTHOUSE
NEAR MARYLAND PARKWAY &
SAHARA

Las Vegas, NV 89104
(866) 670-4443
(702) 312-4625
Fax: (702) 312-4627

Guesthouse for gay men. No restrictions on nudity. 5 rooms, one suite (suite has private bath, rooms share bath). Pool, hot tub, sunbathing. Breakfast included.

NEVADA

LUCKY YOU BED AND BREAKFAST

Las Vegas NV 89104-1547
(702) 384-1129
Fax: (702) 384-1129
Website: www.theinnkeeper.com/bnb/7416

Guesthouse for gay men. Entire house, garden, and pool is clothing optional. 4 bedrooms with king and queen beds and 2 baths, one with whirlpool. Oldest gay owned B&B in Las Vegas. Close to the strip and gay bars. TV, VDR, Videos. Pool, hot tub, outdoor shower. Full American breakfast and other meals catered to you by Liberace's former chef. Near nude beach at Lake Meade, Grand Canyon and other southwestern wonders near by. Private sightseeing to Hoover Dam, Lake Meade, and the strip. Airport pickup available.

NEW HAMPSHIRE

NUDE CLUBS / GROUPS / ORGANIZATIONS

NEW HAMPSHIRE NATURALLY (NHN)

Box 132
Elkins, NH 03233-0132
Contact: Clark R. (603) 526-4309
Email: NHbare4u@aol.com

Approx. 55 members
Membership only newsletter
Yearly dues: $ 20 per year
Potential members welcome
Unlimited attendance
1 party per month (no fee for members, $2 for non-members)
Events include: indoor/outdoor, potluck, movie night, theme/holiday, river/beach,
guest speakers, massage, shaving, safe sex demonstrations

NEW JERSEY

NUDE CLUBS / GROUPS / ORGANIZATIONS

NEW JERSEY BARES (NJB)

PO Box 440
Berkeley Heights, NJ 07922-0440
(201) 444-4953
Email: njbares@hotmail.com
Website: www.meetup.com/New-Jersey-Bares/

Yearly dues: $15 single / $25 couple
Potential members welcome
1-2 parties per month (fee)
Events include: regular indoor, buffet dinners, theme/holiday

CLOTHING-OPTIONAL ACCOMMODATIONS

OCEAN HOUSE

127 S Ocean Ave
Atlantic City NJ 08401-7202
(609) 345-0198
Website: www.oceanhouseatlanticcity.com

Guesthouse with intimate atmosphere for gay men only. 15 rooms (14 with shared baths, sink in each room). 200 yards from the boardwalk. Nudity permitted anywhere with no restrictions. Reservations not taken over the phone.

NUDE BEACHES / RECREATION AREAS

SANDY HOOK – AKA GUNNISON BEACH
(IN THE GATEWAY NATIONAL RECREATION AREA)

Probably the most popular nude beach for the Middle Atlantic states, with a large gay following. The nude section is posted (yes, legally).

DIRECTIONS: Take the Garden State Parkway to Exit 117; then take Route 36 east to Sandy Hook (about 12 miles). At Sandy Hook, follow the signs to North Beach. Park in lots "G" or "H" or near the Old Gun Battery (about 5 miles from the park entrance). The nude area is about 1/4 mile south of the parking area along the beach.

Alt. Directions: From New York City (Manhattan), take the Ferry from the World Trade Center. Ferry runs from just before Memorial Day to just after Labor Day. $20 round trip fare. Take $1 shuttle to area "G".

Our Last Report: Sandy Hook

Fire Island is nice, Jones Beach and Long Beach are too, but if you live anywhere near New York City or The Jersey Shore, Sandy Hook represents the best choice for getting naked for a variety of reasons. First and foremost, getting naked is what it's all about, but getting there is half the battle, especially for the naked enthusiast living in the New York City area. All the other above-mentioned beaches are more than an hour away. As most city dwellers depend on public transportation, the usual drill involves over-crowded trains, then busses, then a long walk to the secluded area where one can gain exposure.

The other option is that offered by our Federal government, just across the Hudson River and adjacent to the Garden State. It is called Sandy Hook and is part of the
Gateway National Recreation Area on the Jersey Shore. Sandy Hook is the largest nude beach on the East Coast and has been for the past 30 years.

And getting there is half the fun. Step aboard the Ferry, offered by New York Waterway, and you begin your trip with a lovely boat ride across the mouth of the New York Harbor. A schedule of morning departures and afternoon return trips are available by calling NY Waterway at (800) 53-FERRY. Enjoy a snack or beverage en route and arrive to a waiting shuttle to spirit you to one of six ocean beaches and three bay beaches, which cover miles of clean and pristine ribbons of sand. Given the hasslefree ease with which the ferry runs, the fun begins before you get there.

Besides offering exquisite city views of the Statue of Liberty and New York City in the distance, this is a living, protected habitat offering fishing, hiking and bird watching, but Gunnison Beach is the part of Sandy Hook that readers of Naked Magazine will want to focus on. There is enough beach for everyone. So it's never crowded like Jones and, while there are definite sections for gay and straight, there is no definitive line between them; instead there is just an indefinable area where people are just people, naked body and soul.

The season officially begins on Memorial Day Weekend and ends Labor Day Weekend. Besides being one of the most beautiful and pristine beaches (on a par with anything Malibu, California might offer), what is so great is the legitimacy offered to the naturist. As this land is owned and operated by the National Parks Service and the U.S. Department of the Interior, nudity is not only sanctioned, it's catered to. Lifeguards are on duty from 10:00 until 5:00 p.m. every day and park rangers patrol the sand. It's kind of fun sitting there naked and having a patrolman with a warm smile walk up and say, "Hi."

Feel like a hot dog or a grilled cheese sandwich and some fruit? How about a beer or soft drink? Hot dogs, pizza, sandwiches and other goodies are also available. It's really nice to stand and gab with other naked folks who are in line to order various snack bar items and watch the counter people not even blink an eye as they hand you your change. Wanna bring back something to your non-nudist partner? Sloganed souvenirs and T-shirts are sold. Some advice might be to have a waist pouch with you for your money. There are also clean and modern bathroom and shower facilities.

The beach is unusual in that there is a long sandbar that separates part of the beach from where the waves break, creating a kind of long wading pool with a soft sand bottom. You can recline on the sandy slope facing the beach with the water between you. It's just a lovely place. Another difference is the people. Even though one can argue that the folks who live and frolic at other beaches nearby are the same ones who come to Sandy Hook, it's like the magical element of this place changes the general atmosphere and a geniality permeates the air like a spell. Come with friends, or make some. Bring your non-nudist partners and they'll feel welcome, too. A good time is always had by all.

Some rules of etiquette which also happen to be Federal laws at this site are:

- Bring it in, take it out. This means whatever you bring to the beach that will be trash at the end of the day (soda cans, food wrappers, newspapers, and other trash) you must take home with you and dispose of there. The park supplies paper trash bags at the boardwalk for your use. Do not leave them on the beach, at the snack area, or in the rest room facilities. Leave the beach in its natural state and you avoid having to pay a hefty fine if you are caught.

- Man's best friend is better left at home. No pets of any kind are allowed on the beach.

- "No resting near nesting for officers are arresting." You should definitely stay out of the dunes and bird nesting areas. These are protected areas and you could be arrested.

- Please read all postings. Stay to the right of the ATTENTION signs unless you are clothed.

- Use proper restroom facilities.

- No photographs or videos.

- Illegal substances are not allowed.

- There are park rangers on patrol at all times.

- Obey lifeguards and swim only in posted swimming areas.

NEW MEXICO

NUDE CLUBS / GROUPS / ORGANIZATIONS

NAKED AND NOT ASHAMED
C/O DON SCHRADER

1810 Silver SE Apt B
Albuquerque, NM 87106
Contact Don S. (505) 843-6595

No newsletter
No yearly dues
Events include: naked conversations

CLOTHING-OPTIONAL ACCOMMODATIONS

CASA MANZANO

103 Forest Rd
Tajique, NM 87016
(505) 384-9767
Fax: (505) 384-9766
Email: casa.manzano@earthlink.net
Website:
www.home.earthlink.net/~casa.manzano

Overlooking a range of mountains, this lodge is miles from the nearest neighbor but only an hour from the Albuquerque airport. A luxury B & B in an elegant Southwest home, it features a hot tub, a full gym with a tanning bed, fireplaces, hiking trails and rooms that open on a garden courtyard. Great food, cordial hosts and home-made bake goods guarantee an unforgettable visit.

INN OF THE TURQUOISE BEAR

342 East Buena Vista Street
Santa Fe, NM 87505
(800) 396-4104
(505) 983-0798
Fax: (505) 988-4225
Email: bluebear@newmexico.com
Website: www.turquoisebear.com

A bed and breakfast mostly for gay men. 9 rooms (7 with private bath), 2 suites with private baths. Nudity permitted in patio and balcony. Breakfast and afternoon refreshment included.

NUDE BEACHES / RECREATION AREAS

MANBY HOT SPRINGS —
AKA STAGECOACH HOT SPRINGS
(ARROYO HONDO, NM)

On the ruins of an old stagecoach stop, this set of three soaking pools is nestled on the banks of the Rio Grande. The largest of the three can hold about ten people. Some gay men frequent this area and, as with all public places, be sure of the climate for tolerance of nudity before completely disrobing (on occasion this site is used by families, etc.).

DIRECTIONS: From Taos, go take US-64 west about 4 miles to the junction with NM-522. You must turn left in order to stay on US-64. After this junction, continue for approximately 4 miles. Just past the airport turn on the left, look for the turnoff on the right. Turn right after the blue metal building onto a gravel road called Tune Drive. Bear left at the fork (about 5 miles) and continue bearing left. You will reach a parking area above the river gorge. From the left corner (as you're looking at the river) there's an established trail. The springs are about a 15 minute hike on this trail.

PRIDE GYM
(ALBUQUERQUE, NM)

1803 3rd Street NW
Albuquerque, NM 87102-1411
(505) 242-7810
Email: pridegym@aol.com

Private men's health club with free weights, machines, cardio equipment, steam room, sundeck with Jacuzzi, tanning beds, personal trainers, massage, health-food bar and lounge areas. Members may sunbathe nude on the sundeck and clothing is optional in the outdoor Jacuzzi. Day, week, and month passes available for non-members.

SPENCE HOT SPRINGS
(BETWEEN LA CUEVA AND JEMEZ SPRINGS, NM)

A traditionally cruisy area where nude bathing is common (and even posted). The rock pool can hold 10 people and the rocks are great for sunning.

DIRECTIONS: North on US-285 from Santa Fe approximately 16 miles to Pojoaque. Make a left onto NM-502 and continue about 20 miles to Los Alamos. The route changes to NM-501. Stay on NM-501 for six miles past Los Alamos. Turn right at NM-4 junction. Look for junction with NM-126 in La Cueva Pass this junction and stay on NM-4 for about one and a half miles. Park in the parking area on the left. There is a trail from the parking area that crosses a log bridge over the Jemez River. After going up a steep slope you will reach the springs.

TEN THOUSAND WAVES
(SANTA FE, NM)

This is a commercial Japanese health spa that offers both private and public hot tubs and saunas. Nudity is permitted in communal areas during the day, but bathing suits are required at night. This site is popular with many, including gay men.

DIRECTIONS: Going south from Santa Fe on I-25, take Exit 282 and go north on St. Francis Drive (US-84) into town. After 3.6 miles make a right onto Paseo de Peralta (this street actually crosses I-84 twice. Be sure you don't take it the first time it intersects. Continue to Washington Avenue and turn left. After a short distance on Washington Avenue, make a right onto Artist Road which changes into Hyde Park Road. A little over 3 miles down the road is Ten Thousand Waves.

NEW YORK

NUDE CLUBS / GROUPS / ORGANIZATIONS

IN THE BUFF (ITB)

4016 Main St. Rd. #15
Batavia, NY 14020
Email: inthebuff@reb-online.com - lsheldon@adelphia.net

Approx 50 members
Yearly dues
Unlimited attendance
Potential members welcome
Inquire by mail
Monthly Meetings

MALES AU NATUREL (MAN)

332 Bleecker St Box 133
New York, NY 10014
(212) 898-0383
Contact: Michael S.
Email: man@males.org
Website: www.males.org

Members-only newsletter
Yearly dues
Limited attendance
Potential members welcome
1 party per month (fee)

NORTHEAST NUDE SOCIETY (NNS)

PO Box 8402
Endwell, NY 13762-8402
(570) 756-2007
Email: nnshilside@aol.com - nnshillside@stny.rr.com
(New York address, but landed in Pennsylvania)
Contact: Phil

Approx 170 members
Members-only newsletter
Yearly dues: $30 single / $50 couple
Unlimited attendance
Potential members welcome
1 party per month (no fee)
Events include: outdoors, camping

CLOTHING-OPTIONAL ACCOMMODATIONS

BELVEDERE GUESTHOUSE

33 Bay View Walk
Cherry Grove, NY 11782
(631) 597-6448
Fax: (631) 597-9391
Website: www.belvederefireisland.com

A guesthouse for gay men on Fire Island. 40 rooms (10 with shared baths). Pool, whirlpool. Near nude beach. No restrictions on nudity.

COLONIAL HOUSE INN

318 W. 22nd St.
New York, NY 10011
(800) 689-3779
(212) 243-9669
Fax: (212) 633-1612
Email: houseinn@aol.com
Website: www.colonialhouseinn.com

Bed and breakfast in a 20 room Brownstone in the heart of Gay Chelsea New York. Some rooms with shared and some with private bathrooms. Clothing optional on rooftop sundeck. Massages available. Transportation available. 24 hour Concierge.

GROVE HOTEL

PO Box 537
Sayville, NY 11782
(631) 597-6600
Email: reservations@GroveHotel.com
Website: www.grovehotel.com

Gay hotel near 4 bars with disco on property. 60 rooms. Pool, beach nearby. Nudity permitted at the beach. Near Fire Island infamous meat rack — "The Woods".

HILLSIDE CAMPGROUNDS

PO Box 726
Binghamton, NY 13902
After April (570) 756-2007
Email: info@hillsidecampgrounds.com
Website: www.hillsidecampgrounds.com

Campgrounds for gay men only. Nudity allowed throughout the grounds. Campsite facilities included: electric/water hook-up at all sites, small cabins, pool, RV units for rent. Storage lockers and camp store.

HOTEL 17

225 E 17th St
New York, NY 10003
(212) 475-2845
Fax: (212) 677-8178
Email: hotel17@worldnet.att.net
Website: www.Hotel17NY.com

Nude sunbathing on roof. Gay men and women welcome. 200 rooms with shared baths. European style. No pool.

JONES POND CAMPGROUND

9835 Old State Rd
Angelica, NY 14709
(585) 567-8100
Fax: (585) 567-2524
Email: info@jonespond.com
Website: www.jonespond.com

117 acre campground for gay men only. Nudity at the pool and most of campground. Events every weekend plus a DJ & Dancing in a 2,000 SF dance barn. Heated pool, cabins, guesthouse, 175 sites with water & elec. Large RV friendly. Seasonal May 1 to Oct. 1.

PINESPLACE

PO Box 5309
Fire Island Pines, NY 11782
(631) 597-6162

Gay guesthouse with fire places, ocean view rooms. Nudity permitted. Summer only.

NUDE BEACHES / RECREATION AREAS

CHAUTAUQUA GORGE
(WESTFIELD, NY - NY/PA BORDER)

This skinny-dipping site has an area designated nude by locals. You'll know you've reached the nude area by the painted rocks. Pools for soaking and areas for sunning along the creek are available and Skinny Dip Falls is just one mile from the end of the trail.

> *DIRECTIONS:* In Westfield, take exit 60 off I-90 and head south on NY-394 (left). Turn right onto US-20. After crossing the bridge, take the first left onto Taylor Road (unmarked - not paved). Follow to the dead end sign and continue (4-wheel drive would be best at this point). Park in parking area and continue on foot. Head downstream until you see the painted rocks declaring nude use.

CHERRY GROVE AND FIRE ISLAND PINES
(FIRE ISLAND, NY)

Highly popular nude beaches with largely gay use. Fire Island is a low slung barrier reef south of Long Island. It can be reached by ferry, or by private boat or charter seaplane.

> DIRECTIONS TO PASSENGER FERRY: Take I-495 (Long Island Expressway) east through Nassau County to Suffolk County. Take Exit 59 (8 miles past junction with Sagtikos State Parkway) and go south on CR-93. Continue to Sayville. Look for signs to ferry dock.

JONES BEACH
(NEAR LONG BEACH, NY)

Popular with straight and gay beachgoers. Part of Jones Beach State Park.

> *DIRECTIONS:* Take the Meadowbrook Pkwy south to Jones Beach. Park in Field 6 and walk east along the beach for about 30 minutes to nude area.

POINT O'WOODS
(FIRE ISLAND, NY)

Not as gay as Cherry Grove or The Pines. Clothed and unclothed sunbathers generally coexist without any problems.

POTTER'S FALLS — AKA SIX MILE CREEK
(ITHACA, NY)

College students from Cornel University and Ithaca College can be found at this site. Though not particularly gay-associated, it is a beautiful skinny-dipping area. A large waterfall and rocks for sunning are its best features. Rangers are tolerant of nude bathing.

> *DIRECTIONS:* Go southeast on State Street in Ithaca (NY-79). At the junction of NY-366, continue past intersection and look for Water Street. Turn right onto Water Street, then left onto Giles Street. Continue to the end of the street and park. Follow the trail at the end of the road. You may encounter nude bathers at the dam, but continue to find Potter's Falls.

ZOAR VALLEY BEACH
(NEAR BUFFALO, NY)

Tradition since the 60s has kept this beach nude. It's a little difficult to get to and be sure to bring something to lie on (the "beach" is shale).

> *DIRECTIONS:* Take US-62 south from Buffalo to Gowanda (about 25 miles). When you come to a 5-way intersection, turn left onto South Water Street. Stay on this street for three quarters of a mile; it changes names twice due to sharp turns (Commercial Street and Palmer Street). Turn right onto Broadway Road and go up the hill just under one mile. Turn left onto Point Peter Road. After 1.8 miles the road will turn sharply left. Veer right and turn onto an unmarked road (called Forty Road). After you cross an iron bridge you will come to a parking area. Hike downstream of the Cattaraugus Creek for a mile. A half mile downstream on the left side there is a trail through the woods that follows the creek. The beach is where the two forks of the creek some together. Your feet will get wet on this hike!

NORTH CAROLINA

NUDE CLUBS / GROUPS / ORGANIZATIONS

CAROLINA SUN FOXES (CSF)

3504 Grimes Ave.
Durham, NC 27703
Email: sunfoxes2004@aol.com

Approx 75 members
Members-only newsletters
Yearly dues
Potential members welcome
1 party per month

METROLINA BUFFS CLUB (MBC)

PO Box 3182
Fort Mill, SC 29708-3182
(Club meets in Charlotte NC)
(803) 322-4763
Email: tkoro@earthlink.net - tkoro@cetlink.com
Website: www.groups.yahoo.com/group/metrolinabuffs

OHIO

NUDE CLUBS / GROUPS / ORGANIZATIONS

CENTRAL OHIO NUDE GUYS ALLIANCE (CONGA)

PO Box 323
Plain City, OH 43064
(614) 447-7190
Email: conga1825@aol.com
Website: www.congaline.org

Approx 110 members
Members-only newsletter
2 parties per month (fee)
Seeking to expand membership
Events include: indoor/outdoor, potluck, pool/hot tub, movie night, theme/holiday.

NORTH EAST OHIO NATURISTS (NEON)

PO Box 770911
Lakewood, OH 44107
(216) 556-4856
Email: information@neonnaturists.org
Website: www.neonnaturists.org

Approx. 125 members
Public newsletter
Yearly dues: $30 single / $50 couple
Attendance set by host of event
Potential members welcome
1-3 parties per month (fee)
Events include: potluck, pool/hot tub, movie night, theme/holiday, exercise/aerobics, massage exchange, bondage/shaving

SOUTHERN OHIO NATURIST SOCIETY (SONS)

PO Box 19371
Cincinnati, OH 45219
Email: CintiSONS@hotmail.com
Website: www.g-hosting.info/sons/
Potential members welcome

OKLAHOMA

NUDE CLUBS / GROUPS / ORGANIZATIONS

CENTRAL OKLAHOMA MALE NATURISTS (COMN)

PO Box 780323
Oklahoma City, OK 73178-0323
Email: comnaturists@yahoo.com

Approx. 12 members
COMN is a private club created to provide an outlet for social and recreational gay male nudity in a non-sexual context among the men of Central Oklahoma.

NORTHEAST OKLAHOMA NUDISTS (NEON)

Tulsa, OK
Email: neonmen@hotmail.com

Group started in late 2000
Approx. 25 members
Guests are always welcome
Activities include: pool parties, Halloweenie costume party, charades and Bingo, and a "Who Wants to be a Naked Millionaire" game night.

CLOTHING-OPTIONAL ACCOMMODATIONS

AMERICA'S CROSSROADS B&B RESERVATIONS SERVICE

P.O. Box 270642
Oklahoma City, OK 73137
(405) 495-1111
Fax: (405) 943-8289
Email: acbbrso@aol.com
Website:
www.inntravels.com/usa/ok/rdac.html

Bed and breakfasts (3 properties: Warren House, Executive Home, and White Cottage). Hot tub at Warren House, pool and hot tub at Executive House. Nudity permitted in pool and hot tubs at night (also discreetly during the day).

OREGON

NUDE CLUBS / GROUPS / ORGANIZATIONS

OREGON MEN ENJOYING NATURISM (OMEN)

PO Box 4941
Portland OR 97208-4941
(503) 234-3943
Email: omenpdx@omenpdx.com
Website: www.omenpdx.org

Group is 2 years old
Approx. 30 members
Meets third Sunday of each month
Guests are always welcome

NUDE BEACHES / RECREATION AREAS

INNER CITY HOT SPRINGS
(PORTLAND, OR)

This is a commercial hot tub/spa facility with clothing-optional status encouraged by owner. A popular place for gay men, but straight men and women also use the facility. Nudity is permitted in the pool, sauna, and sundeck areas.

DIRECTIONS: 2927 NE Everett in Portland. Phone (503) 238-4010 or (503) 238-1065.

KENO ROAD ROCK QUARRY
(ASHLAND-MEDFORD AREA, OR)

A large pond formed by a natural spring that flooded an excavation site. Maintained by volunteers from The Rogue Suncatchers, a local nude group. Very popular and draws many gay men.

> *DIRECTIONS:* Ashland is fourteen miles north of the California border. Take Exit 14 off I-5 in Ashland and go east on OR-66 for one mile. Turn left onto Dead Indian Highway and drive for seventeen miles. Keno Access Road is on the right (almost 2 miles past the Howard Prairie Reservoir turn). Turn right onto the road and drive to the top of the hill to the gravel piles. Turn right onto the dirt road. Drive around the quarry's edge to the parking area.

ROOSTER ROCK STATE PARK
(ROOSTER ROCK, OR)

Rooster Rock is a very traditional clothing-optional beach area on the Columbia River, patrolled by a park staff, with a boat launch and picnic tables. It has been clothing optional for as long as anyone can remember because it is not illegal to be naked in public in the state of Oregon. It has lots of parking (for a fee) and miles of sandy beach.

> *DIRECTIONS:* Rooster Rock State Park is 20 miles east of Portland on Interstate 84. The clothing-optional area is marked with signs. Just drive in the main gate and turn right (east). Follow to the end of the parking lot, where you'll find a restroom. About 40 feet from the rest room is a stairway. Draw an imaginary line along the stairway down to the river and up the bank and to the south. The sanctioned clothing-optional area is on the east end of that line.

SAUVIE ISLAND GAME REFUGE
(NEAR PORTLAND, OR)

Used by gay and straight nudists.

> *DIRECTIONS:* From Portland, take Highway 30 north to Sauvie Island Bridge. Take Reeder Rd. for about 4 miles past Social Security Beach. Watch for two trails leadingto the river.

PENNSYLVANIA

NUDE CLUBS / GROUPS / ORGANIZATIONS

PHILADELPHIA AREA NAKED GUYS (PANG)

PO Box 42691
Philadelphia, PA 19101-2691
Contact: (215) 978-PANG (7264)
Email: For Email, please go to web page
Website: www.PhillyNakedGuys.org

Newsletter, Yearly dues, Potential members welcome

CLOTHING-OPTIONAL ACCOMMODATIONS

CAMP DAVIS

311 Redbrush Rd
Boyers PA 16020
(724) 637-2402
Email: campd@aol.com
Website: www.campdaviscampground.com

Clothing-optional, membership-only campground on 22 secluded acres. Swimming pool, hot showers, toilets, recreation hall, dancing, volleyball, games, hiking and more!

RAINBOW MOUNTAIN RESORT

210 Mt. Nebo Road
East Stroudsburg, PA 18301
(570) 223-8484
Website: www.rainbowmountain.com

Guesthouse for men only. Clothing-optional poolside. 1 mile from Rainbow Mountain.

ONEIDA CAMP & LODGE

East Lake Rd, Ste Route 1012
PO Box 537
New Milford PA 18834
(570) 465-7011
Fax: (570) 465-2521
Email: information@Oneidalodge.com
Website: www.oneidacamp.com

Oneida Camp, located on 100 acres at the Top of the Endless Mountains of Northeastern Pennsylvania, is the oldest gay-owned and operated campground dedicated to the gay community. Entire camp is clothing-optional. 12 rooms includes 2 cottages with kitchens, 14 rooms with shared bathrooms and Kitchens and 2 sleeping cabins with refrigerators, sauna and clubhouse. Membership fee of $5.00 each year.

RHODE ISLAND

NUDE CLUBS / GROUPS / ORGANIZATIONS

GAY RHODE ISLAND NUDISTS (GRIN)

PO Box 643
Forestdale, RI 02824-0643
(401) 766-9670
Email: nkdm4m@aol.com
Members-only newsletter

NUDE BEACHES / RECREATION AREAS

MOONSTONE BEACH
(NEAR PROVIDENCE, RI)

A nude beach frequented by both straight and gay nudists.

> *DIRECTIONS:* Take Route 4 from I-95. It will become Route 1 after traffic circle. Exit at the sign for Trustom Pond National Wildlife Refuge (a U-turn will be necessary) onto Moonstone Beach Rd. You can park (for a fee) at Roy Carpenter's Beach.

SOUTH CAROLINA

NUDE CLUBS / GROUPS / ORGANIZATIONS

THE CAROLINA BUFFS (NC & SC)
C/O WALT G

109 Prince Dr, Ridgeway, SC 29130-8487
(803) 337-8511
Email: thecarolinabuffs@naturalmales.org

Approx 35 members, Members-only newsletter, Yearly dues: $10 single
Potential members welcome, Events include: indoor/outdoor, potluck

METROLINA BUFFS CLUB (MBC)

PO Box 3182, Fort Mill, SC 29708-3182
(Club meets in Charlotte NC) - (803) 322-4763
Email: tkoro@earthlink.net
Website: www.groups.yahoo.com/group/metrolinabuffs

CLOTHING-OPTIONAL ACCOMMODATIONS

HEIGHT OF FOLLY

1309 E Ashley Ave
Folly Beach, SC 29439
(843) 588-6200

Apartment on Folly Beach for gay men only. Nudity permitted on sundeck and in hot tub.

NUDE BEACHES / RECREATION AREAS

FOLLY BEACH
(NEAR CHARLESTON, SC)

The northern tip of Folly Island is a discreet nude beach for gay men. Police will visit, but they can usually be spotted approaching with plenty of time for you to cover up.

DIRECTIONS: Take Exit 216 from I-26 and head south on SC-7 for approximately 2 miles. Bear left onto SC-171 (also called Folly Road). Stay on SC-171 for approximately 10 miles until you reach the town of Folly Beach. SC-171 becomes Center Street after crossing onto Folly Island. Turn left onto East Ashley Avenue and take that road to the end. Park at the Folly Beach parking area (fee charged). Walk right and around the end toward the intercoastal Waterway.

SOUTH DAKOTA

CLOTHING-OPTIONAL ACCOMMODATIONS

CAMP MICHAEL B&B

13051 Bogus Jim Road
Rapid City, SD 57702
(605) 342-5590

A bed and breakfast with gay and lesbian clientele. 4 rooms and bunkhouse. Nude sunbathing permitted on sundeck (subject to comfort level of other guests) and in hot tub (clothing prohibited in hot tub). Nude hiking also is a possibility here. (Gay owned and operated)

NUDE BEACHES / RECREATION AREAS

HIPPIE HOLE
(SOUTH OF RAPID CITY, SD)

A traditionally nude spot with no reports of a strong gay presence. Due to its proximity to Mount Rushmore and the fact that it is the only report of a nude beach in South Dakota, we thought we'd list it here for those visiting the area.

DIRECTIONS: Take US-16 south from Rapid City for 12 miles. In Rockerville, turn left onto CR-C233 (South Rockerville Road) and continue approximately three miles. Just before the cattle guard, turn left onto a gravel forest road (FS-372). Just over one mile there are two dirt roads to your right. Take the second dirt road. After another 3/4 mile you will come to another cattle guard. After the cattle guard, bear right twice over the next .3 mile or so to a small circular parking area. Take the trail to the river - about a fifteen minute hike.

TENNESSEE

NUDE CLUBS / GROUPS / ORGANIZATIONS

TENNESSEE NATURIST CLUB (TNC)
C/O D DRAKE

2167 Hillsboro Heights
Knoxville, TN 37920
(865) 577-5260 Ext 4
Email: taxman99@prodigy.net - taxman@comcast.net

TENNESSEE AREA NATURISTS (TAN)

PO Box 2332
Brentwood, TN 37024-2332
615-791-7572
Email: tnareanaturist@yahoo.com

Approx. 70 members
Members-only newsletter
Yearly dues: $15 single / $30 couples
Potential members welcome
1 party per month
Events include: indoor/outdoor, potluck, pool/hot tub

CLOTHING-OPTIONAL ACCOMMODATIONS

TIMBERFELL LODGE

2240 Van Hill Rd
Greenville TN 37745
(800) 437-0118
(423) 234-0833
Fax: (423) 434-8512
Email: timberfell@timberfell.com
Website: www.timberfell.com

Guesthouse for gay men. Entire facility is clothing-optional. Swimming pool with beer bar, spa, exercise room, and tavern on premises. Main lodge accommodates 14 and has 2 private baths. Annex building has 10 rooms (4 with private baths). 30 camp sites, 14 RV hook-up sites. 250 acres to roam around naked.

TEXAS

NUDE CLUBS / GROUPS / ORGANIZATIONS

AUSTIN GAY NUDISTS (AGN)

PO Box 684101
Austin, TX 78768-4101
(512) 933-9464
Email: AustinGayNudists@excite.com

Approx. 85 members, Members-only newsletter
Yearly dues: $20 single / $40 couples
Potential members welcome, 1 party per month
Events include: indoor/outdoor

BEXAR MEN (PRONOUNCED "BARE")

PO Box 12342
San Antonio, TX 78212-0342
Contact: Joe (210) 223-6189
Email: bexarmen@hotmail.com
Website: www.bexarmen.org

Members-only newsletter, Yearly dues
Unlimited attendance, Potential members welcome
1 party per month

DALLAS AREA MALE NATURISTS (DAMN)

PO Box 190869
Dallas, TX 75219-0869
(214) 521-5342 Ext 1739
Email: dallasmen@swbell.net - cchasdal@sbcglobal.net
Website: www.DAMNmen.org

Approx. 100 members
Yearly dues: $25 single / $40 couples
Membership only newsletter
1-2 parties per month (fee)
Events include: potential member parties, indoor/outdoor, potluck, pool/hot tub, movie night, theme/holiday, naked photo shoots with models

LONE STAR NUDIST GROUP (LSNG)

PO Box 66621
Houston, TX 77266-6621
(713) 866-8847
Website: www.lsnghouston.com

NORTH TEXAS AREA NATURISTS (NORTH-TAN)

2001 Aden Rd. #200
Fort Worth, TX 76116
Website: www.northtexasnaturists.com

CLOTHING-OPTIONAL ACCOMMODATIONS

PARADISE GUESTHOUSE

2317 Bernardo de Galvez (Ave P)
Galveston Island, TX 77550
(877) 919-6677
(409) 762-6677
Fax: (409) 763-3406
Email: paradiseEL@aol.com

Paradise guest house and Oh! Susana's serves the gay and gay friendly community in the true spirit and look of Key West, Acapulco and Hawaii, New Orleans and, of course, Texas. Our inviting complex sits nestled within walking distance to beaches, bars, shopping and restaurants. Accommodations designed for most every budget. All of our accommodations are near the pool, spa and patios with clothing optional in pool areas only. 5 beautiful suites and 4 lovely rooms. Impressive Island décor. Cable TV with VCR, video library, refrigerator, comfortable seating and a queen sized beds. Some suites have full kitchens.

THE SUMMIT HOUSE

1204 Summit St
Austin TX 78741
(512) 445-5304
Email: summit@texas.net

Bed and breakfast serving gay and straight clientele. 3 rooms (one with private bath). Nudity permitted in sunbathing areas and indoors. Breakfast included. Walking distance to downtown. Massage and tours available.

THE NEW UPPER DECK HOTEL & BAR

POB 2309
120 E. Atol Street
South Padre Island, TX 78597
(956) 761-5953
Fax: (956) 761-4288
Email: spiup@aol.com

Guesthouse for gay men and women. Nudity permitted in courtyard/patio areas, hot tub areas (2), TV room and game room. G-string or more required by pool when the bar is open. Inquire with management about nude sunning when bar is closed. 15 rooms with private baths, 6 semi-private (shared bathroom), a kitchen living area and 4 of the 6 share 2 bathrooms. All have AC & Cable TV plus one Adult channel. Rooms in adjacent buildings also for rent (formerly duplex housing). Continental breakfast included. Located at the southern tip of Texas on the Gulf of Mexico. Beautiful tropical beach setting. The hotel is located in popular resort area of South Padre Island. It's a small town atmosphere with plenty of restaurants, bars, shops and activities for vacationers. The town thrives on the tourist industry.

NUDE BEACHES / RECREATION AREAS

HIPPEE HOLLOW AT LAKE TRAVIS — AKA MCGREGOR PARK (AUSTIN,TX)

A popular nude beach with a separate gay area. It is legal to get naked here and the ranger at the parking booth will tell you so. There are three times in the year when you will find hoards of gay men at Hippie Hollow: First Splash, Last Splash, and Meltdown (Memorial Day and Labor Day events - First Splash can be earlier in May). All three of these are Austin area "circuit parties" that have a large number of gays who party on barges in the lake. Nude use during these times is strange - only some of the guys take the nude option at Lake Travis - the others keep their suits on. Any other time of the year, this is a great place to get naked! There is no sandy beach, so come prepared to lie on the rocks.

DIRECTIONS: Take FM 2222 from Austin to FM 620. Continue on FM 2222 straight through the intersection about a mile and turn left at Oasis Bluff Road. Continue until it ends, turning right on Comanche

Trail. Continue about a mile; Hippie Hollow Park Entrance (fee) will be on the left. Gay men gather at the far right end. Caution: don't dive from the limestone ledges as the lake bottom depths near the shore are very irregular.

BARTON CREEK GREENBELT (AUSTIN, TX)

Several locations are frequented by nude visitors along the creek. The creek runs through Austin, but it provides many secluded areas for nude bathing. Twin Falls is the popular place for skinny dipping.

DIRECTIONS: Take Riverside west from I-35 to Barton Springs Road. Turn left and follow road to Zilker Park. Entrance to greenbelt is in the park.

SOUTH PADRE ISLAND (SOUTH PADRE ISLAND, TX)

by Shane Andrews, Travel Editor

Often, when folks think of the state of Texas, the last image conjured up would be a nude beach. Actually, the Lone Star State is pretty tolerant toward those of us who like to get "nekked." South Padre Island is one such place where nudity is not only practiced, but is also legally tolerated.

South Padre Island is a very popular Spring Break destination for mid-western college students. So if you're not looking for hoards of drunken co-eds or like to sit in hours (yes, hours) of traffic, I would suggest avoiding this Texan paradise during the month of March. Oh yes, and if you're thinking of catching a glimpse or two of some naked college boys, braving the crowds most likely will not be worth your while. Nearly all the Spring Breakers stay on the developed part of the island during their week of mayhem and few (if any) make it to the nude beach.

There is a dune buggy rental shop on the main street of the island. If you are planning a visit to the nude beach on South Padre, you will be best served in a four-wheel drive vehicle or a dune buggy. You must drive quite a distance on the beach to reach the nude section. Depending on conditions, this invites disaster for most two-wheeled vehicles. Play it safe and use the appropriate vehicle. You don't want to ruin your day by getting stuck in the sand. In the event you do get stuck, there is often a local person with a truck looking to make extra money (sometimes a LOT of money).

There are a couple of ways to approach the nude section of the beach on South Padre Island. Some take the main road until it ends then continue driving on the sand. I found that even a four-wheel drive vehicle has trouble with this route.

You may make it, but it's questionable. The sand at the end of the road is usually very soft and not at all packed down. The easier way is to exit the road at Beach Access Point #6 (the last beach access before the road ends). For the summer months, this access point is graded and drivable, but if you're on the island before that time, you're better off taking Beach Access Point #5 (a year-round access). There is a fee of $3.00 for entering at the access point and you will receive a trash bag for your garbage. There was a time at Access #6 when you could return a full trash bag for a partial refund of your entrance fee.

Once you've driven onto the beach at Access Point #5, turn left and drive approximately 10 miles north on the beach. Throughout the years, the beach has been marked many ways. Local rumor has it that it used to have a sign posted by park rangers simply stating, "Nude Sunbathing Permitted." But, as you can imagine, this was a popular theft item. Then for a long time there was a large driftwood log with the word "NUDE" painted on it with white paint.

During my last trip, there was a barrel way off to the left toward the dunes marked with the word "nude" and two miles farther north from that were two more markers - one old oil tank declaring "nude" (more visible than the last barrel) and directly on the shore line a huge, orange, metal object that looked as though it were a piece of a crashed rocket (someone told me it was a buoy anchor) with the words "Nude Beach" spray painted on it. On a weekday you may be the only person on the beach for miles, so as soon as you've driven a reasonable distance north, you can simply disrobe where you are.

South Padre Island beach offers great sea shell hunting and the dunes are not restricted. Also, at this point the island is so narrow you can climb to the top of a dune and easily see the bay side of the island from where you stand. Some people camp on the beach here, and there are no signs restricting this activity. If you should decide to camp, you should be aware that there are wild coyotes on the island. There has never been a report of them causing any trouble, but I wouldn't want you to be as shocked as I was the first time I saw some on a foggy day!

The water in the Gulf of Mexico gets extremely warm during the summer. As a matter of fact, don't look for a dip in the water to be very refreshing in August. In general, however, the beach here is quite peaceful and untouched. The water is usually clean (depending on when the last storm churned the waters) and the beach is extremely peaceful. This is not a place to go if you are seeking large group nudity. You will see other nude bathers, but folks who use this beach tend to set up their spots with lots and lots of space between them and the next bathers (after all, you have the entire north end of the island!). This section of the island is also popular with off-shore fisherman due to the fewer number of swimmers disturbing the fish.

If you're looking for a good gay nude beach for cruising, this beach is not for you. There has been some minimal cruising on the beach and in the dunes, but remember: this is a nude beach enjoyed by all and is not a gay-only nude beach. Also, if you like your privacy while bathing and don't appreciate gawkers, you may want to set your area up in the dunes. When lying directly on the beach you have to contend with the occasional "passer-by" who will be driving farther north on the beach. Traffic on the beach is not usually heavy, but it's always a good idea to look both ways before going into the water!

There are no vendors or amenities close by, so if you're going to make a day of it, be sure to pack plenty to drink and any other food or comforts you may require. As I mentioned earlier, this section of the island is very isolated and untouched. There are very rare occasions when you will see a ranger patrol the beach. I've never seen one personally, but I have naked friends who have and they said they didn't bother to cover up. They just waved and the ranger waved back, which further solidifies the sanctioned status of this nude beach.

The weather on South Padre Island is warm nearly all year and can get extremely hot during the summer months. Rain is rare, but does happen occasionally. As when planning a trip anywhere, it's good to check the weather before you go. December and January can get cold, but I have seen very warm days during these months. In February and March the weather can be changeable.

As far as other local attractions, Brownsville, Texas is about forty-five minutes drive from the island and many people like to go shopping in Matamoras, Mexico (across the river from Brownsville). There is one gay bar in Brownsville, shopping, restaurants, and a nationally ranked zoo (Gladys Porter Zoo). There is also a gay nightclub in Harlingen, Texas which is a short drive from the island.

Gay accommodations on the island can be found at The New Upper Deck guesthouse. It is located in the downtown section of the island so you can stay close to the nude beach in a gay facility. The guesthouse has a pool, Jacuzzi, and a gay bar on the premises. Nudity is permitted in the Jacuzzi and around the pool (when the bar is closed). More recently, a gay-friendly motel has opened called South Beach Inn but you'll need to stay clothed in the open areas of this property.

If you are looking for a peaceful nude beach getaway, South Padre Island may be just the place for you. Most of the year it is not crowded, the weather is warm, and the people are very friendly. Enjoy some Tex-Mex hospitality!

> *DIRECTIONS:* There are a few ways to get to the nude beach on South Padre Island. One is to take the paved road (main drag on the island, TX-100) all the way to the end. Drive off the road and continue up the beach (north) for about 5 miles or so. The sand is always very soft here, so you will need a four-wheel drive vehicle with high clearance. The second route (easier on your vehicle but 4-wheel is still recommended for driving on the beach) is to take the paved road only to beach access point 6 (the last beach entrance before the end

of the road) or access point 5. After paying the small fee at the booth turn left on the beach and drive to the nude area (you'll see the first marker approximately 10 miles from the entrance of Beach Access Point #5. There are NO facilities on this beach, so take everything you need and be sure to clean it all up before you leave.

UTAH

NUDE CLUBS / GROUPS / ORGANIZATIONS

UTAH MEN ENJOYING NATURE (UMEN)

PO Box 16128
Salt Lake City, UT 84116-0128
(801) 532-7472
Email: plumwine@earthlink.net
Website: www.umen.org

NUDE BEACHES / RECREATION AREAS

THE MARSH — AKA SARATOGA SPRINGS (NORTHWEST OF PROVO, UT)

Do not confuse this with the springs at Saratoga Resort (nearby). Hot spring pools and some hot mud spots can be found here. This area can be cruisy for gay men.

> *DIRECTIONS:* From Provo take I-15 north and exit onto UT-73 at Lehi. Go west on UT-73 to UT-68, then turn left onto UT-68. Turn left at West 6800 North Street and after a short distance there will be a T intersection with Saratoga Road. Park and walk to the springs.

VERMONT

NUDE BEACHES / RECREATION AREAS

HUNTINGTON GORGE
(NEAR BURLINGTON, VT)

The pools formed by the creek attract nude bathers. There are foundations of an old mill on the opposite side of the shallow creek that is popular with gay men.

> *DIRECTIONS:* Take Exit 11 off I-89 south (from Burlington). Take US-2 east to Jonesville. About three tenths of a mile past the Jonesville Country Store, turn right onto Stage Road. Cross Winooski and Huntington Rivers. Stage Road is now Cochran Road. After the Huntington River, veer left onto Dugway Road (may not be marked). About a mile up this road there are parking pullovers and trails leading to the river from the left side of the road. The last parking area is closest to the gay area.

JEFFERSONVILLE GORGE — AKA BREWSTER RIVER
FALLS (NEAR BURLINGTON, VT)

Nudity is traditional upstream from the park. Popular gay nude site farther upstream.

> *DIRECTIONS:* Take Exit 15 from I-89 and go northeast on VT-15 to Jeffersonville. Pick up VT-108 and head south toward Smugglers Notch and Stowe (you'll be on this road for less than one mile). Look for a restaurant with a waterwheel. Take the first left which leads to a covered bridge. Turn right on the small dirt road just before the bridge. Park in the parking area and take the trail to the river. To get to the nude area you will need to wade (the trail ends at the river and continues on the other side).

THE LEDGES
(WILMINGTON, VT)

This area of granite outcroppings off the Harriman Reservoir is perhaps the most popular nude site in New England. Summer weekends can draw hoards of nudists - many of them gay.

DIRECTIONS: From I-91 take Exit 2 and go west on VT-9 toward Wilmington. Make a left on VT-100 (a mile before Wilmington). Just over one mile, bear right onto a dirt road labeled "NEPCO Picnic Area" and continue about a mile. Park as far north as possible and take the trail. The gay section is north of the central nude area.

MIDDLEBURY RIVER GORGE
(MIDDLEBURY, VT)

Popular with gay men. Most people just sunbathe by the creek.

DIRECTIONS: Take US-7 south about three and a half miles. Turn left onto VT-125 and then left onto the dirt road just before the concrete bridge that crosses the Middlebury River. After one and a half miles, park on the side of the road and wade across the creek.

ROCK RIVER
(NEAR BRATTLEBORO, VT)

There are several pools formed by Rock River; the third and fourth pools upstream are gay and nude. The trail leading from the first to third pool is about a mile and can be cruisy.

DIRECTIONS: Take VT-30 north from Brattleboro. Parking is available one and a half miles from the Maple Valley ski area. Walk across the road onto Williamsville Road and walk uphill for a half mile. Cross over the guardrail on the right side of the road and take the trail to the river.

SILVER LAKE
(NEAR SALISBURY, VT)

A small lake in the Green National Forest. The area has primitive toilet facilities and a sandy beach and camping is permitted. Nudity is common at Silver Lake, the Falls of Lana, and the trail to Rattlesnake Ridge. Popular site with gay men.

> *DIRECTIONS:* Take US-7 north to Brandon, then go east on VT-72 to the village of Goshen. Turn left on VT-32 (paved but pavement ends and road is gravel). After two and a half miles turn left onto FS-27. Take the right fork after three quarters of a mile and continue to the end of the road.

VIRGINIA

NUDE CLUBS / GROUPS / ORGANIZATIONS

RICHMOND AREA NUDE GUYS (RANG)

PO Box 26601
Richmond, VA 23261
Email: rangmembership@aol.com

SOUTH EAST AREA MEN ENJOYING NATURISM (SEAMEN)

3208-106 Holland Rd Box 931
Virginia Beach, VA 23456
(757) 424-NUDE
Email: Seamen2000@hotmail.com

Members-only newsletter
Approx 150 members
Yearly dues
Meet every 3 weeks
Potential members welcome
Activities include cookouts, massage, hot tub parties and theme nights, parties
with other clubs.

WASHINGTON

NUDE CLUBS / GROUPS / ORGANIZATIONS

THE OLYMPIANS
C/O T CLEMENTS

823 NE 80th St
Seattle, WA 98115
Voice Mail: (206) 405-2013
Email: olynewsletter@aol.com
Website: www.TheOlympians.net

Approx. 146 members, Members-only newsletter
Yearly dues: $18 single / $28 couple, Attendance number per host
Potential members welcome, 2 parties per month (food/guest fee)
Events include: indoor potluck, hot tub

CLOTHING-OPTIONAL ACCOMMODATIONS

TRIANGLE RECREATION CAMP

Mountain Loop Highway
Silverton, WA
Email: info@camptrc.org
Website: www.camptrc.org
Directions: 21 miles past Granite Falls, WA,
on the Mountain Loop Highway, 1 mile before
Silverton,WA.

Nudity allowed everywhere, except for parking lot, on the highway, or visible to river
travelers. Campers are mostly gay men, some lesbians. Must be gay or lesbian to
camp at the campground. Age requirement is 21.

NUDE BEACHES / RECREATION AREAS

COOPER POINT — AKA EVERGREEN BEACH (NEAROLYMPIA, WA)

Used predominantly by students of Evergreen State College. Most of the bathers are men with a large percentage of them gay. Don't be nude on or close to the trail (you'll upset campus security).

DIRECTIONS: Take Route 101/401 from I-5 to the campus. Take Cooper Point Dr. to Driftwood. Park in Lot F. Trail to the beach is at the rear of the lot. Bear to the right at each fork of the trail.

HIGH BRIDGE/PEOPLE'S PARK — AKA LATAH CREEK BEACH (NEAR SPOKANE, WA)

There is a firmly established local tradition of nude use here. This beach draws a mixture of nudists and is popular with gay men.

DIRECTIONS: About a 15 minute walk from downtown Spokane. Head west on Riverside Ave. until Riverside intersects with Clarke near the Spokane River. Walk about 400 yards to the forested area until you come to the parking lot near the junction of Hangman Creek and the Spokane River. The nude beach is located where Latah Creek joins the Spokane River.

POINT WELLES — AKA RICHMOND BEACH
(RICHMOND BEACH, WA)

Since Carkeek Park sustained much flood damage, the nudists in the Seattle area have migrated here. A popular gay site, but last report says that straight nudists are using it more.

DIRECTIONS: From downtown Seattle, go north on I-5 and take the exit for 175th Street. Go west on 175th Street for approximately one mile, turn right onto Aurora Avenue and continue about three quarters of a mile. Turn left at 185th Street, which will turn into Richmond Beach Road. At the T intersection at the end of the road, take a right and park before the gate to the oil tanks. Go north on foot to the end of the road, then take the trail to the train tracks. Follow the tracks (about 10 minutes) then take the trail just past the fence that surrounds the oil tanks.

WEST VIRGINIA

NUDE CLUBS / GROUPS / ORGANIZATIONS

WEST VIRGINIA MOONSHINERS (WVMS)

PO Box 5333
Charleston, WV 25316
(304) 345-6934
Email: wvmoonshiners1999@aol.com
Website: www.wvmoonshiners.homestead.com

Meetings on the first Saturday of the month.

CLOTHING-OPTIONAL ACCOMMODATIONS

ROSELAND GUESTHOUSE & CAMPGROUND

Rd1, Box 185B
Proctor WV 26055
(304) 455-3838
Email: info@roselandwv.com
Website: www.roselandwv.com

222 secluded acres catering to gay men, with scenic, mountain-top views, guest rooms, cabins, seasonal trailer sites, campsites, food service, store, theme weekends, pool, 2 hot tubs, and hiking. Clothing optional. Bar on premises.

WISCONSIN

NUDE CLUBS / GROUPS / ORGANIZATIONS

WISCONSIN BARES (WB)

PO Box 8066
Gurnee, IL 60031-8066
(847) 248-0098
Email: whitefox3302@yahoo.com

Approx. 160 members, Public Newsletter
Yearly dues: $20 single/ $30 couple, Limited attendance
Potential members welcome
1 party per month (fee)
Events include: indoor

CLOTHING-OPTIONAL ACCOMMODATIONS

PRAIRIE GARDEN BED & BREAKFAST

W 13172 Highway 188
Lodi, WI 53555
(800) 380-8427
Email: prairiegarden@prairiegarden.com
Website: www.bnblist.com/wi/prairie

Bed and breakfast. 4 rooms with private baths, one deluxe loft cottage suite (private bath) with full kitchen. Nudity permitted in hot tub. Breakfast included. Near Mazo Nude Beach. Full country breakfast.

NUDE BEACHES / RECREATION AREAS

MAZO NUDE BEACH
(NEAR MADISON, WI)

This beach is located in the Mazomanie State Wildlife Refuge and is sanctioned for nudity although recent reports say it is facing the ups and downs of attention that most nude areas face. It is popular with both straight and gay nudists with a larger portion being men. The water is too shallow to swim in, but beach activities are common and there is enough water to wade in and cool off. We are told that the nude area changes as the Wisconsin River changes path. Once there, just look for the naked people!

> *DIRECTIONS:* On the Wisconsin River about 14 miles west of Madison in the Mazomanie State Wildlife Refuge. Take County Y for 4 miles and turn right onto Laws Drive. Follow Laws Drive until you see the gravel road. The nude beach is near where the cars park. Canoes are available for rent locally for nude canoeing ("canuding").

UNITED STATES

TERRITORIES

PUERTO RICO

CLOTHING-OPTIONAL ACCOMMODATIONS

VILLA BOUGANVILLA

Box 258
Vieques, PR 00765
(787) 643-2411
(787) 741-1049
Email: info@viequesislandcasa.com
Website: www.viequesislandcasa.com

Private villa and casita on island off the coast of Puerto Rico. Entire villa must be booked by same party. No restrictions on nudity.

US VIRGIN ISLANDS

CLOTHING-OPTIONAL ACCOMMODATIONS

SAND CASTLE ON THE BEACH

127 Smithfield
Predriksted, St. Croix, USVI 00840
(800) 524-2018
(340) 772-1205
Fax: (340) 772-1757
Email: info@sandcastleonthebeach.com
Website: www.sandcastleonthebeach.com

Resort hotel for gay men and lesbians. 19 rooms, 7 suites, 8 apartments, 2 luxury villas, and 2 pools. One pool is clothing-optional and there are secluded beaches nearby.

NUDE BEACHES / RECREATION AREAS

ST. JOHN - SOLOMON BEACH

Unpopulated, small, secluded beach with a small gay presence.

DIRECTIONS: Located on national park land on the west coast of St. John, this beach is within walking distance from Cruz Bay (the main town). Walk along Lind Point trail, which starts behind the visitor's center, and hike along the hillside until you get to an unmarked but well-worn fork of the trail that descends to Solomon Beach.

ST. THOMAS - LITTLE MAGEN'S BEACH

Remote beach on the north coast of St. Thomas popular with gay men.

> *DIRECTIONS:* Walk 15 minutes from Magen's Bay along the water's edge (to the right). The beach is secluded by rocks – inquire locally about current tolerance level for nudity.

INTERNATIONAL

AUSTRALIA

NUDE CLUBS / GROUPS / ORGANIZATIONS

CAIRNS SUNBOYS (CS)

PO Box 7262
Cairns Queensland 4870 AUSTRALIA
Fax: (+61)-7-4081-0075
Email: sunboys@bigpond.com
Website: www.sunboys.rainbownet.info

GAY SYDNEY AUSTRALIA (GSN)

4 Edinburgh Avenue
Carlingford, NSW 2118 AUSTRALIA
(+61)-2-9683-4102
Email: gsn-gni@buckdale.net
Website: http://groups.yahoo.com/group/gay_sydney_nudists

BRISBANE SUNBOYS
C/O ROBI & COLIN

Box 10439 Adelaide Street P O
Brisbane QLD 4000 AUSTRALIA
Email: sunboys_brisbane@yahoo.com.au

Approx. 50 members
Members-only newsletter
Yearly dues
Unlimited attendance
Potential members welcome
2 parties per month (fee): swim night on each third Sunday and for a BBQ/Pool Party on each first Saturday monthly

GAY NAKED BUDDIES SYDNEY (GNB SYDNEY)

Sydney NSW AUSTRALIA
+61 415 353 996
Email: gnbsydney@hotmail.com
Website: www.gnbsydney.net

Gay Naked Buddies (GNB) Sydney is a gay nudist social group for youthful guys, who are fit and active, in Sydney, NSW, Australia.

CLOTHING-OPTIONAL ACCOMMODATIONS

ABACA PALMS

34 Whatley Crescent, Mt. Lawley
Perth, Western Australia, WA 6050
Australia
(+61) 8 92 712 117
Fax: (+61) 8 93 715 370
Mobile: 0422 425 119
Email: info@abacapalms.com
Website: www.abacapalms.com

Perth's only gay B&B. Enjoy a Spa and Sauna. Large 10-seat salt water, heated Jacuzzi. Large Art Deco character house with 7 bedrooms. Nudity permitted. Only 6 minutes from the city center by public transport.

BEACH PARADISE

PO Box 26
Vincentia, NSW 2540
Australia
(+61) 2 4443 7047
Email: sdupee@hotmail.com

THE HILL HOMESTEAD

No. 2 Kiora Rd
Bingara, NSW 2404
Australia
(+61) 2 6724 1686
Fax: (+61) 6724 1381
Email: thehill@northnet.com.au

HIGH TWEETERS HOLIDAY FARM

Nullo Mountain
Rylstone NSW 2849
Australia
(+61) 2 6379 6253

18-24 JAMES

18-24 James St
Cairns, QLD 4870
Australia
(+61) 7 40 514644
(+61) 7 40 510103

Designed around the pool and spa, 18-24 James offers 26 hotel rooms plus shared accommodations. Features include nude sunbathing, pool, spa, gym and much more.

SKINNY DIPS RESORT AND SPA

4870 Queensland
PO Box 1845
Cairns, QLD 4870
Australia
(+61) 7 40 514 644
1-800-62-1824
(Toll Free within Australia)
Fax: (+61) 7 40 510 103
Email: enquiries@skinnydips.com.au
Website: www.skinnydips.com.au

Plantation-style gay guesthouse in northern Australia with 21 guest rooms. Cairns is set in a tropical rainforest close to Barrier Reef. Near whitewater rafting and beaches, as well as bustling restaurant and casino nightlife. Each room has its own private bathroom, ceiling fans, A/C and television. Pool, spa, sauna and gym. Nudity permitted poolside.

BUSH HOUSE BED AND BREAKFAST

PO Box 282
West Burleigh 4219
Australia
(+61) 7 55 338 408
Email: info@bushhouse.net
Website: www.bushhouse.net

Totally private and exclusively gay secluded bed & breakfast in the natural bush surroundings of the gold coast. Unwind by the pool or in the spa, soak up the sun (clothing optional), or fire up the barbeque.

BALCONIES DAYLESFORD

35 Perrins Street
Daylesford, VIC 3460
(+61) 3-53-481-322
Fax: (+61) 3-53-481-322
Email: info@balconiesdaylesford.com
Website: www.balconiesdaylesford.com.au

Bed and breakfast for gay men and women. 4 rooms. Indoor pool, sauna, and whirlpool. Nudity permitted in sunbathing area and pool room.

FALCONS AT PEREGIAN

P.O. Box 254
Pergian Beach, QLD 4573
Australia
(+61) 7 5448 3710
Fax: (+61) 7 5448 3712

Bed and breakfast for gay men. Pool and gym. No restrictions on nudity. Continental breakfast included.

GOVERNORS ON FITZROY

64 Fitzroy Street
Surry Hills NSW 2010
Australia
61-2-9331-4652
Fax: 61-2-9361-5094
Email: info@governors.com.au
Website: www.governors.com.au

Guesthouse with mostly gay male clientele. Gay women welcome. Nudity permitted on sundeck and spa area. 6 rooms with shared baths. All with vanity sinks. Restored terrace house with two lounge areas, including 24 hour coffee/tea.

MANYANA

51 Kestrel Crescent
Peregian Beach, QLD 4573
Australia
(+61) 7 5448 2010
0418 747 088 (mobile)

Motel for gay men. Pool and gym, with beach nearby. Nudity permitted at pool and all fenced areas.

MENGYUAN BED AND BREAKFAST

200 Woodswallow Drive
Gin Gin Qld 4671
Australia
+61(7) 4157-3024
Email: admin@mengyuan.com.au
Website: www.mengyuan.com.au

Bed and Breakfast for gay men and women. Nudity permitted in spa area.

THE OASIS ON FINDERS

106 Flinders St.
Darlinghurst NSW
Australia
(+61) 2 9331 8791
Fax: (+61) 2 9332 2247
Email: admin@oasisonflinders.com.au
Website: www.oasisonflinders.com.au

Sydney's only bed & breakfast retreat for gay male nudists with three large guest rooms, and a small sun deck and whirlpool, right near the action on Oxford street. Grand three-story Victorian terrace.

PARADISE RETREATS

102 Admiralty Drive
Surfers Paradise
Gold Coast, QLD 4217
Australia
(+61) 7 5571 1414
Fax: (+61) 7 5531 0614

A guesthouse for gay men. 5 rooms (2 with private baths). Pool, whirlpool. No restrictions on nudity. Breakfast included.

SWANBORNE GUESTHOUSE

5 Myera Street
Swanbourne 6010
Perth Western Australia
(+61) 8 9383 1981
Fax: 8 9385 4595
Email: info@swanbourneguesthouse.com.au
Website:
www.swanbourneguesthouse.com.au

Luxurious guesthouse for gay men and gay women. Sundeck and sunbathing area. Close to gay nude beach. 4 rooms with self-contained kitchens, some with private baths. Quiet and private.

TURTLE COVE RESORT

Captain Cook Highway
POB 158
Smithfield Cairns, QLD 4878
Australia
(+61) 7 4059 1800
Fax: (+61) 7 4059 1969
Email: gay@turtlecove.com.au
Website: www.turtlecove.com.au

Resort complex for gay men and gay women. Located on private, clothing-optional beach. 31 rooms, all with private baths, restaurant, pool, spa, sun deck, cocktail bar and minigym. Gay reef and rainforest tours. Check the Website for details of Nude Week held May each year.

NUDE BEACHES / RECREATION AREAS

ALEXANDRIA BAY
(NEAR NOOSA HEADS, QUEENSLAND)

One of the most popular beaches in Queensland. Has strong gay following.

DIRECTIONS: Tourist maps available in Noosa (Noosaville, Noosa Junction, and Noosa Heads) show the locations and access points.

BUCHANS POINT
(NEAR CAIRNS, QUEENSLAND)

Just north or Cairns, this is a popular, unofficial nude beach especially with gay men.

DIRECTIONS: From Cairns, go north on the Cook Highway for about twenty-five kilometers. Look for a parking lot on the right side of the highway, about a half kilometer north of Palm Cove Resort and before Ellis Beach. The nude area is south past a large rock.

KAMBAH POOL
(AUSTRALIAN CAPITAL TERRITORY)

A natural pool in the Murrumbidgee River, this is the most popular inland nude beach in the country. Entirely rock with some flat areas for sunbathing, this beach is popular with everyone and has a gay contingent.

DIRECTIONS: From Canberra, take Route 23 south to Tuggeranong. Turn right onto Sulwood Drive, then turn left onto Kambah Pool Road. Go through the roundabout at Berritt Street to the lower parking lot, and then walk about 200 yards downstream to the nude beach.

CASUARINA FREE BEACH
(NEAR DARWIN, NORTHERN TERRITORY)

Nude sunbathing occurs at the northern end. Frequented by gay men. Swimming at Casuarina Beach isn't possible during the Australian Summer (wet season November-April) because of the highly poisonous jellyfish, called sea wasps or stingers which are present in high concentration. Their venom is among the most poisonous of all venomous creatures! As an added bonus, there may be saltwater crocs as well. In other words, don't get in the water here, though you may be able to check the danger level with locals.

DIRECTIONS: From Darwin, head northwest toward the airport on Stuart Highway. Just past the race track, turn left onto Bagot Road which becomes Talbot Road. Go past McMillans Road. Turn right onto Trower Road then turn right onto Casuarina Drive and go to the beach parking area. Nude area is posted.

LADY JANE BEACH
(NEAR SYDNEY, NSW)

Located in Watson's Bay in the spectacular Sydney Harbor area and not on the ocean. It is officially nude and very popular with gay men. The rocky area on the ocean side is quite famous for cruising.

DIRECTIONS: From Sydney, take Route 76 (New South Head Road) where it will become Hopetown Avenue and then head north to Watsons Bay. In Watson's Bay, turn left onto Military Road. Park near Cliff Street. Walk behind the military reserve to Camp Cove and look for the sign for the beach.

LITTLE CONGWONG BEACH
(NEAR SYDNEY, NSW)

The main beach, Congwong Beach, is popular with families. Little Congwong Beach is right next to it. It's not officially nude, but many of the beachgoers are nude. The smaller beach is good if you want privacy.

DIRECTIONS: From Sydney take Anzac Road south to the village La Perouse. There is a parking lot just south of the village. Steps lead down to the beach.

MASLIN BEACH
(NEAR ADELAIDE, SOUTH AUSTRALIA)

Legal nude beach popular with gay men. A beautiful beach 3 km long, Maslin Beach is considered to be one of the best nude beaches in Australia. The nude area is along the south end.

DIRECTIONS: Go south, through Morphet Vale, on Main South Road for about 45 km. Turn right onto Sandpits Road, then left at next intersection. Go south for several kilometers, turn right onto Tuit Road, go past the Maslin Beach Caravan Park and park in the cliff-top parking area.

NORTH SWANBORNE BEACH
(NEAR PERTH, WESTERN AUSTRALIA)

A very popular beach with a long history of nude use. The gay section is away from the crowds. Stay out of the sand dunes behind the beach. The sand is extremely hot and the dunes are sometimes patrolled by the police.

DIRECTIONS: Take the Stirling Highway southwest from Perth and turn right at Eric St. and right again at Marine Parade. Follow the road to the car park. The nude area is about 300 meters north. Watch for poisonous snakes in the area!

NORTH SUNNYSIDE BEACH
(NEAR MELBOURNE, VICTORIA)

A popular official nude beach on the Mornington Peninsula and the closest nude beach to Melbourne. The gay section is at the far end of the beach, towards Mt. Eliza.

DIRECTIONS: From Melbourne, take the Nepean Highway (Route 3) south. 8 km south of Frankston, look for the sign to Sunnyside Beach.

OBELISK BAY
(NEAR SYDNEY, NSW)

Another harbor beach near Mosman in northeast Sydney. It's not officially nude, but it's small, somewhat secluded and mostly used by and popular with gay nudists.

DIRECTIONS: From Sydney cross the Harbour Bridge and turn northeast on Route 14 (Military Road). After one and a half kilometers, turn right onto Belmont Road. Follow the road several kilometers and make a left on Middlehead Road. Just after Middlehead Road turns into Chowder Bay Road, Take the first right turn and park. Take the trail downhill to the beach.

POINT IMPOSSIBLE
(NEAR MELBOURNE, VICTORIA)

A popular official nude beach. The gay section is at the end of the beach.

DIRECTIONS: Take Route 1 west from Melbourne through Geelong. Just outside of Geelong and before Torquay, turn left on the road to Breamlea. Just before the end of the road, turn left to Black Gate Road, drive to the end and park.

SHEELY BEACH
(NEAR BALLINA, NSW)

A beautiful cove, located just north of Ballina, at the mouth of the Richmond River.

DIRECTIONS: Look for a paved road just after the first residential subdivision. The north end is usually used by nudists and gay men. Not an official nude beach.

SHELLEY BEACH
(TOWNSVILLE, QUEENSLAND)

Townsville is near the popular gay resort town of Cairns. This is a popular nude site though it is an unofficial nude beach.

DIRECTIONS: From Townsville, head north on the road to Pallarenda (pass through Belgian Gardens and Rowes Bay). Continue until you reach the public park at the end of the road. Park and take the trail to the beach. Walk past the clothed section and at low tide you can walk around the rocks to the nude area. Otherwise you will need to climb the rocks.

SOMERS BEACH
(NEAR MELBOURNE, VICTORIA)

An unofficial nude beach near the town of Somers on Western Port Bay, about 75 km southeast of Melbourne.

DIRECTIONS: From the car park at the beach, follow the track down to the water and then walk along the beach for about 2 kilometers past the "Commonwealth Property" sign.

WARNBRO BEACH
(NEAR ROCKINGHAM, WESTERN AUSTRALIA)

Some people say that this beach is officially nude, others say it's not. Either way, it gets a lot of nude use. It has clear water, gentle waves and a clean beach. The afternoon winds are usually strong, most visit in the morning.

DIRECTIONS: From Rockingham, take Safety Beach Road south, then Fendham St. until you reach the north 3 car park. The nude area is 1 km to the south, at the far end of the beach.

WASHAWAY BEACH
(NEAR SYDNEY, NEW SOUTH WALES)

A beach that draws smaller crowds, but it is heavily gay. Being used as an alternative site since Reef Beach was declared non-nude.

DIRECTIONS: From Sydney, cross the Harbour Bridge and turn northeast onto Route 14 (Military Road). At Pit Junction, follow Spit Road north over Spit Bridge, then go right onto Sydney Road to Balgowlah. From there, go right onto Condamine Street. Continue and look for signs for Sydney Harbour National Park. The beach is located off Cutler Road in Balgowlah Heights.

WERRONG BEACH
(STANWELL PARK, NEW SOUTH WALES)

A legally nude beach south of Sydney. Popular with all nudists, especially gay men.

DIRECTIONS: From Sydney, go south on Route 1 (Princess Highway) to the F6 Freeway. Follow the signs east toward Stanwell Park, then turn left to Otford Lookout. Go past the sign for Royal National Park and continue to parking on the right past the sign for the Otford Railway Station. Follow the trail labeled Burning Palms Clifftop Walk and Werrong Beach. Take the fork to the beach when the trail splits. The decent to the beach is steep and takes about 30 minutes.

AUSTRIA

NUDE CLUBS / GROUPS / ORGANIZATIONS

AUSTRIAN GAY NATURISTS (AGN)

Email: naturist@gay.or.at
Website: www.naturist.gay.or.at

NUDE BEACHES / RECREATION AREAS

DANUBE ISLAND — AKA DONAUINSEL (NEAR VIENNA)

A narrow island formed by the Danube and the manmade "New Danube," which is popular with gay naturists. The nude sections are at the north and south ends.

DIRECTIONS: Best if reached by bus, ferry, or subway since parking in this area is a problem.

FORST SEE (NEAR VELDEN)

A popular nude beach that is on a small lake in the woods (once a quarry).

DIRECTIONS: From Velden, go east on the main highway about three and a half kilometers along the north shore of Wörther See. At the aluminum works, turn left and go about one and a half kilometers, then go left about 400 yards and park on the side of the road at Forst See.

HAWAII BEACH
(NEAR INNSBRUCK)

On the Inn River just west of Innsbruck, this beach is popular with gay men though not a legal nude beach. The nude section is to the west.

DIRECTIONS: Best way to get there is to take the bus. Take LK or K to the final stop. From the bus stop, cross the street and go to the river. Walk to the right (facing river) to reach a large green field - this is the nude beach.

KEUTSCHACHER SEE
(NEAR KLAGENFURT)

This beach is right next to a large nudist campground and is popular with gay men.

DIRECTIONS: From Klagenfurt, go south on Route 91 and follow signs to the west for the southern shore of Wörther See, the large lake that extends several kilometers toward Villach. Go west along Wörther See and look for signs to Keutshacher See.

BARBADOS

NUDE BEACHES / RECREATION AREAS

LONG BEACH
(NEAR CHRIST CHURCH)

Just south of Grantley Adams International Airport. The two-mile stretch of beach is popular with gay men. Watch for patrol men (spotted easily) and be ready to cover up.

> *DIRECTIONS:* Take the bus that goes to Inch Marlowe to the end of the line, then walk a mile or so northeast (left when facing water) to reach the nude area. If traveling by car, park at the Long Beach Club and walk northeast about a half mile.

BRAZIL

NUDE BEACHES / RECREATION AREAS

PRAIA BRAVA
(CABO FRIO, RIO DE JANEIRO)

Once was officially clothing-optional, but fanatics have gotten the status changed. It remains a popular nude site.

DIRECTIONS: North of Porto Veliero in Cabo Frio, near Japanese Island. Park at Nacil Bar and walk about 1,000 feet to the nude beach.

PRAIA DO PINHO
(NEAR CAMORÍU, SANTA CATARINA)

This is a legal nude beach (Pine Beach) on the Atlantic coast of the southernmost area of Brazil. Draws many gay men.

DIRECTIONS: From Florianópolis, go about 70 kilometers north along the coast on Highway 101. Turn right onto a dirt road near kilometer marker 140. The road leads 8 kilometers to the beach. You can take a bus from Florianópolis if you like.

PRAIA TAMBABA
(NEAR CONDE, PRAÍBA)

A legal nude beach on the Atlantic coast. Large beautiful beach with clear water, white sand, and lots of palm trees.

DIRECTIONS: Bus excursions from Joâo Pessoa and dune buggies can be rented in Recife and Conde.

CANADA

NUDE CLUBS / GROUPS / ORGANIZATIONS

GAY OTTAWA NUDISTS UNDER THE SUN (GO-NUTS)
C/O 169 CRICHTON STREET

Ottawa, ON CANADA K1M 1W1
(613) 237-9872 Ext 2109
Website: www.groups.yahoo.com/group/ottawa_gonuts

PACIFIC-CANADIAN ASSOCIATION OF NUDISTS (P-CAN)

PO Box 530
1027 Davie Street
Vancouver, BC V6E 4L2 CANADA
Contact: Frank C. (604) 669-7977
Email: contact@p-can.org
Website: www.p-can.org (Updated: monthly)

Approx. 270 members, Members-only newsletter Yearly dues, 2 parties per month (no fee): a house party and the very popular Naked Heaven bar night. Guests may attend up to two events, usually free of charge, before having to join the club. Out-oftown guests are welcome. Please contact the club president beforehand. Most house parties are potlucks. BYOB. A "games room" sometimes is available.

SOUTH WESTERN ONTARIO NUDISTS (SWON)
C/O BENSON S.

350-1580 Adelaide St. N
London, ON N5X 2L5 CANADA
(519) 434-7018
Email: gniswon@yahoo.com

Approx. 35 members
Members-only newsletter
Yearly dues: $15 single / $30 couple
Potential members welcome
1-2 parties per month
Events include: indoor/outdoor, potluck, movie night, speakers, discussions

TOTALLY NAKED TORONTO MEN ENJOYING NUDITY
(TNT! MEN)

PO Box 19
552 Church St
Toronto, Ontario M4Y 2E3 CANADA
Hotline: (416) 925-9872 Ext 3010
Email: tnt@tntmen.org
Website: www.tntmen.org

Membership Fee: $20 / year
Approx. 350 members, with between 6 and 10 events each month, including 2 nude swims, nude parties, coffee nights, gallery openings, visits to the theatre, weekend retreats, days at our nude beach (Hanlan's Point) and a wide variety of other events both indoors and out.

CLOTHING-OPTIONAL ACCOMMODATIONS

AUBERGE DU CENTRE VILLE

1070 Rue Mackay
Montreal Quebec H3G 2H1
Canada
(800) 668-6253
(514) 938-9393
Fax: (514) 938-1616

Hotel and health club for gay men. 49 rooms, 29 with private baths. Nudity permitted in sauna, garden and on sundeck.

BAIN DE NATURE

125 Lussier
St Alphonse de Granby
Quebec J0E 2A0 CANADA
(514) 375-4765
Fax: (514) 375-4765
Email: kerry@baindenature.qc.ca
Website: www.baindenature.qc.ca

Resort for gay men and open-minded straight men. Entire resort is clothingoptional and open year round. Swimming pool and spa. 3 bedrooms, 1 with private bath. Livingroom with fireplace. Small lake with natural sunbathing and swimming. Some camping. Bilingual, but mostly French-speaking.

THE BLUE EWE

1207 Beddis Rd
Saltspring Island BC V8K 2C8
Canada
(250) 537-9344
Email: blueewe@shaw.ca
Website: www.blueeweislandcottage.com

Resort on private 5.5 acres with ocean view for gay men and gay women. Full breakfast, hot tub, nudity permitted.

BURNSIDE GUEST HOME

139 William Street
Stratford, ON N5A 4X9
Canada
(519) 271-7076
Fax: (519) 271-0265
Email: burnside@burnside.on.ca

Bed and breakfast mostly for gay men. 4 rooms with shared baths. Nudity permitted in whirlpool, on lower level, in Shakespeare Pond area and on nature trails. Many take nude hikes.

CAMPING DU PLEIN BOIS

550 Chemin St Henri, Ste-Marthe
Cté Vaudreuil, QC J0P 1W0
Canada
(888) 459-4646 (Canada and USA)
(450) 459-4646
Fax: (450) 459-4-9417
Email: info@campingpleinbois.com
Website: www.campingpleinbois.com

Gay men only campground and recreation area. Nudity permitted. Dancing, swimming, and restaurant on premises.

DOMAINE GAY-LURON ENRG

R G Grande Terrei
St Francois-du-lac
Cte Yamasaka, QC J0G 1M0
Canada
(450) 568-3634
Fax: (450) 568-2055

Summer resort for gay men. 60 campsites, 2 apartments, 8 cabins, 3 trailers, and chalets. Nudity permitted on island only.

LA CONCIERGERIE GUESTHOUSE

1019 Rue St Hubert
Montreal, QC H2L 3Y3
Canada
(514) 289-9297
Fax: (514) 289-0845
Email: info@laconciergerie.ca
Website: www.laconciergerie.ca

Guesthouse for gay men. Nudity permitted on rooftop sun deck and in spa area. 17 rooms, 9 with private baths.

LE ST CHRISTOPHE GUESTHOUSE

1597 Rue St Christophe
Montreal QC H2L 3W7
Canada
(888) 521-7836
(514) 527-7836
Fax: (514) 526-6488
Email: info@stchristophe.com
Website: www.stchristophe.com

All male clothing-optional guesthouse. Open all year. Antique furnishings and a rooftop sundeck. Rooms with private baths available. Full breakfast.

LE TRAVERSIN

4124 St-Hubert
Montreal, QC H2L 4A8
Canada
(514) 597-1546
(514) 597-0818
Email: travrsin@homeniscience.com

Bed and breakfast for gay and straight clientele. 5 rooms. Nudity permitted in garden (where Jacuzzi is located).

WEST WIND ACCOMMODATION

1321 Pacific Rim
Tofino, BC V0R 2Z0, Canada
250-725-2777
Email: stay@tofinoaccommodation.com
Website: www.tofinoaccommodation.com

Guesthouse for gay men and women, with some straight clientele. 1 suite and 1 cabin (each with private bath). Nudity permitted in gardens, hot tub, and private sun decks.

NUDE BEACHES / RECREATION AREAS

BEACHGROVE BEACH
(TORONTO, ON)

Located where Highland Creek flows into Lake Ontario. This is a lesser-used beach but a good many of the users are reported to be gay.

DIRECTIONS: Go east on Highway 401 (Macdonald-Cartier Freeway) to Scarborough. Take Exit 387 and go south on Morningside Avenue to Lawrence Avenue. Go left through a residential area then past a water treatment plant. Park in the lot at East Point Park at the end of the road. Take the trail on the northeast corner of the lot which runs along the fence around the water treatment plant. When the trail forks at the top of the bluffs, take the main trail (the upper one) and follow it to the mouth of Highland Creek. Climb up the embankment to the railroad tracks. There is a walkway on the railroad bridge. After crossing the bridge, take the path to the beach.

BEACONIA BEACH
(NEAR WINNEPEG, MB)

The southern end of the beach is nude and farther south almost exclusively gay. When the water is high, you may have to wade to get to it.

DIRECTIONS: Take Highway 59 north from Winnepeg about 70 kilometers. Turn left onto PR-500 and drive through Beaconia. When the road curves to the right, take the smaller gravel road that goes straight ahead and continue about 2 kilometers to the parking area.

CEDAR CREEK BEACH — AKA BEAU SEJOUR BEACH (KELOWNA, BC)

On Lake Okanagan, this beach can be very cruisy. It's a very rocky beach, so bring something soft to lay or sit on.

DIRECTIONS: From Highway 97 (Harvey Avenue in Kelowna) turn south onto Pandosy Street. This will become Lakeshore Road. Continue approximately six kilometers where the road will turn sharply to the right at the intersection with Swamp Road. Turn right at the intersection to continue on Lakeshore Road. After slightly over three kilometers, turn right to the parking area (Boy Scout Camp sign means you've gone too far!!) Walk down to the beach on the stairs. The nude section is to the north.

CRYSTAL CRESCENT BEACH (NEAR HALIFAX, NOVA SCOTIA)

The nude section of the beach is on the southern end and is sometimes called "Mackerel Cove." The gay section is farther south along the rocks.

DIRECTIONS: Take Exit 1 from Highway 102 and go south on NW Arm Drive about 5 Kilometers. Turn right onto Old Sambro Road and continue for eighteen kilometers. In Sambro, turn right at the stop sign (at Harts Store) and continue for two and a half kilometers and follow the sign to Crystal Crescent Beach. Park at the first of three beach areas. Walk south along the beach or on the trail about fifteen or twenty minutes to reach the third beach.

HANLAN'S POINT (NEAR TORONTO, ON)

On one of the small cluster of islands on Lake Ontario near Toronto. This beach is legally clothing-optional and is increasing in popularity. Getting naked outside the clothing-optional zone may still get you a ticket, so be sure to stay within the designated nude area.

DIRECTIONS: Take a ferry from the end of Bay Street. From the ferry dock on the western part of the island, take the paved path for about a ten-minute walk to the tennis courts, then turn right and take the sandy path through the playground to reach the beach.

JOHN E. PEARCE PROVINCIAL PARK
(NEAR LONDON, ON)

Gay men gather at the far end of the nude section of this small nude beach. Weather affects accessibility of the beach so watch for rain.

DIRECTIONS: From London, take Highway 401 (Macdonald-Cartier Freeway) southwest for approximately 45 kilometers. Take Exit 149 and head south on Route 8 through Dutton to Wallacetown, then look for signs for John E. Pearce Provincial Park. Park on the lot by the lake. Walk toward the lake, then turn left and follow the trail at the fence. You'll have to climb down a gully to reach the beach. This is steep, hence the weather warning. Once on the beach, walk to the left for about 15 or 20 minutes to reach the nude section.

LAC SIMON
(NEAR OTTAWA, ON)

This beach is between Ottawa and Montreal, but is closer to Ottawa (Duhamel, QC). Site is popular with straight and gay nudists.

DIRECTIONS: From the Montreal area, take Highway 148 west about 100 or so kilometers to Highway 321, which is a few kilometers past Montebello. Turn right on Highway 321 and go north about 40 kilometers toward Duhamel. Park at the public beach in Duhamel. From the beach, walk to the east until you reach Nation Nord River, which flows into the lake. Cross the shallow river to reach the nude area.

LES CHUTES
(NEAR STE-ADÉLE, QC)

The crowd at "The Waterfalls" is almost exclusively gay. Large boulders provide a place to sunbathe.

DIRECTIONS: Take Highway 15 north and take Exit 69 when you reach Ste Adéle. Go right on the road to Ste Marguerite. After approximately 15 or 20 minutes there is a major bike path that intersects the road. A convenience store is on the left and parking area on the right. Park in the lot and walk across the road and then north on the path. Listen for the falls.

MEECH LAKE
(ACROSS THE RIVER FROM OTTAWA)

Beach Report
By Ian Sherwood

If you ever are visiting Canada's Capital, you might just want to check out its nude beach called Meech Lake. This beach is about a twenty minute drive from Ottawa in the Gatineau Park, near the town of Chelsea, Quebec. It is picturesque with ruins of a carbide mill, a waterfall, an old bridge, pillars and lots of places where you can walk around and be in your favorite suit. The land was settled by Thomas Wilson (1860-1915) in 1907. He used Chemical Fertilizers acid to produce phosphate fertilizer. Meech Lake is also known for the Canadian constitutional amendment that failed. My theory has always been that because Canada's first ministers (the Prime Minister and the provincial Premiers) didn't get nude to negotiate the amendment, is the reason for it not succeeding.

The beach is 90% gay and most of them go nude. Although, nudism is not officially recognized on this beach, the police force leaves it alone. The community around also seems tolerant to nudism at the beach. In fact, in my 16 years of going there, I have only been hassled by the police once. I was told to put my swimsuit on and told I could face a fine of $100, however as soon as they left on their motorbikes, it was off with my suit for me. Signs used to be posted saying that nudism was prohibited in Gatineau Park. However, this year I noticed that all those signs had been removed.

Although you would mostly go there in June, July and August, sometimes in April/May and/or September/October there may be days when it is somewhere around 20-24 C and you just might want to go there. The advantage of pre- and post seasons is that there are no bugs, more tourists though. From the second week of May till the end of May (this may vary a bit from year to year) you do not want to even leave the parking lot because the park is infested by black flies. And yes there are mosquitoes and horseflies there, so be sure to put on some bug protection while walking through the woods. I often go around there for nude walks. It is just a good feeling to walk for a good distance without having to worry about your attire. And you can trust on leaving your gear at your spot of rest while you have your walkabout. Another common activity is floating around on your air mattress.

During the summer I like to get there before 9 a.m. I don't have to pay for parking that way and I can get a good rest spot. I usually close the place at around 6 p.m. As soon as I get there I choose my spot for the day, make myself comfortable by taking off my clothes and pumping up my air mattress. I bring a cooler with some pop, beer and a sandwich and I am set for the day. I have my walkabouts, a few floats, talk to people, swim, read, relax and catch some rays. On a hot day, the beach can easily fill up with 40 to 50 people. And the number of rest spots that one can find depends on how high the water level is.

If you ever go to Meech Lake you will agree with me that it is a piece of paradise. You will find that it relieves you from the stresses and hassles of the city and you would want to keep coming back.

DIRECTIONS: From Ottawa take the Nicholas exit off the Queensway going north, follow the signs to Hull, Quebec (Highway 5), Cross the MacDonald Cartier Bridge into Hull, the bridge will filter traffic onto Highway 5. Continue north on the Highway for 12 km. Take the exit off to Chelsea and turn to left and follow the signs to Gatineau Park. There will be signs posted for Meech Lake, follow those until you reach the O'Brien Beach, which is where you park your car (fee charged in mid June until Labor Day weekend after 9 a.m.). Find the path No 36. Take the path up a hill and into the woods. The path leads down a steep incline. There is a wooden bridge at the bottom, cross the bridge and continue along the path, go to the right when the trail forks. Continue several minutes to reach the rocky beach with the old ruins. The total hike from the parking lot to the beach is about 1.5 km (about 20 minutes).

NORTH GLENMORE PARK
(CALGARY, AB)

This is a grass beach on the Elbow River in Glenmore Park. Not a particularly "busy" beach, but almost all male and gay.

DIRECTIONS: From Highway 8 go south on 37th Street SW to the parking lot just before the park entrance. Head west on the hike/bike path to Weselhead footbridge over the Elbow River. Just before the bridge, take the trail on the left. You'll have to crawl through a fence. Take the path through the bushes, wade across a small creek and continue to the open area along the river. Walk past this open area, through more growth. The next open area is the nude beach.

OKA BEACH
(NEAR MONTREAL, QC)

One of the best-known nude beaches in Quebec. Located at the mouth of the Ottawa River, nude users gather on the far east end.

DIRECTIONS: Take Highway 15 north across the Prairies and Mille Iles rivers, then exit and head southwest on Highway 640, which will become Highway 344. The freeway will end after 27 kilometers, near the town of Oka. When the freeway ends, continue several more kilometers and look for the signs to Oka Park, which is on the left side of the road. Park in the lot near the beach and walk to the beach. The nude beach is east (left when facing the water); take the path along the water.

PRIOR LAKE
(NEAR VICTORIA, BC)

A very small lake near Thetis Lake in Thetis Lake Park. No beach but a floating dock used for nude sunbathing. No facilities or services. There are some secluded nude spots if you follow the trail to Thetis Lake (Trillium Trail).

DIRECTIONS: Take Highway 1 north and west about 10 kilometers. Take Exit 8 and head north a short distance on Helmcken Road. Just past Victoria General Ho spital, turn left onto Watkiss Way. Continue until it joins Highland Road. Head north on Highland Road about 2 kilometers until you see a sign that says "No Parking on Pavement." Park and look for the yellow gate to the fire road and a sign for Trillium Trail. About 50 meters farther there is a trail to Prior Lake.

RIVIÉRE ROUGE
(CALUMET, QC)

Draws a mixed crowd of nude bathers. The nude beach is beyond the first rock outcropping.

DIRECTIONS: Take Highway 148 west about 70 kilometers to the village of Calumet. Just past the village, look for a picnic area just before the bridge over Rivière Rouge. Park and walk upstream on one of the paths along the river. Hike past the clothed beach to the second bathing area.

SCARBOUROUGH BLUFFS
(NEAR TORONTO, ON)

The secluded areas below the bluffs are popular with nudists; however, the bluffs are known to be unstable and people have died by getting trapped under collapsed sand. Use beach at your own risk.

DIRECTIONS: Go east on Highway 2 in Toronto. This highway leaves downtown Toronto as Gardiner Expressway and eventually follows Kingston Road. Go east on Kingston Road into Scarborough. After you pass Birchmount Road, turn right onto Glen Everest Road. Shortly after the turn, bear right onto Fishleigh Drive. Look for Scarborough's pumping station, drive between the two buildings and park. Take the trail to the right along the bluffs and descend to the beach when you see the building at the bottom.

THREE MILE BEACH
(PENTICTON, BC)

A small sandy beach that draws mostly men. Gay men tend to gather farther north (away from the parking area).

DIRECTIONS: The beach is on the eastern side of Lake Okanagan. Head north on Naramata Road (toward Naramata). If you can't find signs pointing toward it, you may have to ask directions. Once you are on Naramata Road, head north for two or three kilometers and look for Three Mile Road to the left (there is a restaurant on the corner). Turn left onto Three Mile Road and park in the lot at the end. Take the stairs to the beach and walk north (to the right). The nude section is just past the large willow.

WITTY'S LAGOON
(NEAR VICTORIA, BC)

The nude beach is just past the clothed beach at Witty's Lagoon Park. This attracts a few nude users, many of them gay.

DIRECTIONS: Take Highway 1 northwest about 14 kilometers. Turn left onto Highway 14 and go 4 kilometers. At Colwood, turn left onto Metchosin Road and continue about 5 kilometers to Witty Beach Road (past the entrance to Witty's Lagoon Park). Turn left and park in the lot at the end of the road. Take the stairs to the beach and right past the overhanging trees.

WRECK BEACH
(NEAR VANCOUVER, BRITISH COLUMBIA)

A huge, legal, nude beach that draws very large crowds. The southern end of the beach (near the mouth of the Fraser River) is the gay section.

DIRECTIONS: From downtown Vancouver, follow 16th Avenue westward through Pacific Spirit Park and the University of British Columbia campus all the way to the end of the road at Marine Drive. Follow signs to visitor parking on Main Drive.

CARIBBEAN ISLANDS

CLOTHING-OPTIONAL ACCOMMODATIONS

LE CARBET

18 rue des Alamandas
Anse Mitan
97229 Les Trois Ilets
Martinique, FWI
(+596) 05 96 66 03 31
Fax: (+596) 05 96 66 03 31
Email: info@lecarbet-gaybandb.com
Website: www.lecarbet-gaybandb.com

Bed and breakfast for gay men. 3 rooms (sinks in each, shared showers). Nudity permitted in Jacuzzi, sunbathing areas, and inside the house depending on comfort level of other guests.

NUDE BEACHES / RECREATION AREAS

ANSE TRABAUD
(ST. ANNE, MARTINIQUE)

An established and remote nude beach in Martinique.

DIRECTIONS: Travel south from Ste. Anne toward Les Salines. Look for the turnoff on the left that leads east to La Baie des Anglais. Turn left and continue about 5 kilometers on the rough road to reach the beach. A fee is collected. Walk to the right as you face the water to reach the nude section.

CUPECOY BEACH
(SINT MAARTEN, DWI)

Located close to Maho in the eastern part of Sint Maarten, just south of the French/ Dutch border. The beach is very popular and draws a good number of gay men. Nearly everyone goes nude and the beach is known to be cruisy.

DIRECTIONS: Go west from Phillipsburg on the main road that goes around the island. When you pass Atlantis Casino and the main road turns to the right just past Sapphire Club, go left on the dirt road and park in the lot behind the hotel. Walk west on the beach to reach the nude section.

ANSE DE GRANDE SALINE
(ST. BARTHELEMY, FVI)

This is an unofficial nude beach (nudity is illegal on St. Barthelemy).

DIRECTIONS: A 10-minute drive from the airport at Gustavia. The turnoff is near the east end of St. Jean Bay. Cab drivers know where the beach is.

ORIËNT BAY BEACH
(SAINT MARTIN, FWI)

Very popular nude beach with a significant gay following. Part of the beach is on the property of Club Oriënt, a straight nude resort.

DIRECTIONS: Head west from the airport in Phillipsburg. Go through Marigot and Grand-Case. Turn left at the sign for Club Oriënt.

PLAGE JEAN ROCQUEMONT
(GUADELOUPE)

This nude beach is adjacent to the nude beach of Club Med Caravelle.

DIRECTIONS: From Pointe-á-Pitre go east on RN-4 about 18 kilometers. About 165 feet past the sign that marks the entrance to Club Med Caravelle turn right onto a dirt road. Park on the side of the road near the food and souvenir vendors. Look for a turnstile and go through it to the beach. Walk right as you face the water to get to the nude section.

POINT TARARE
(GUADELOUPE)

A small but legal nude beach that draws a good number of gay men.

DIRECTIONS: From St-François, go east on the route marked "Pointe-des-Châteaux" which will go north of the golf course. From the intersection at the golf course, go 7.2 kilometers to the turnoff for the beach.

COSTA RICA

CLOTHING-OPTIONAL ACCOMMODATIONS

COLOURS COSTA RICA

8-21 H Blvd Rohmoser
POB 341-1200
San Jose, Costa Rica
(877) WEBOOK2 (932-6652)
(786) 428-0208
Email: newcolours@ colours.net
Website: www.colours.net

A guesthouse with mostly gay clientele. Nude sunbathing and swimming allowed. 12 rooms, 10 with private baths.

HOTEL CASA BLANCA DE MANUEL ANTONIO S.A.

Apdo 194-6350
Manuel Antonio, Quepos
Costa Rica
(+506) 777-0253
(+506) 777-1316
Fax: (+506) 777-0253
Email: cblanca@racsa.co.cr
Website: www.hotelcasablanca.com

Hotel for gays and lesbians. 4 rooms, 2 suites, 4 apartments, and one vacation home. 2 pools with poolside bar, sundeck, and tropical garden. Nudity permitted in pool and garden after 3 p.m. Close to Playita.

LA PLANTACION BIG RUBY'S

Apdo 94-6350
Manuel Antonio, Quepos
Costa Rica
(+506) 777-1332
(800) 477-7829 (US and Canada)
Fax: (+506) 777-0432
Email: costarica@bigrubys.com
Website: www.bigrubys.com

Guesthouse for gay men and lesbians. 24 rooms. Pool, hot tub, outdoor showers. Nudity permitted in pool area. Close to Playita.

NUDE BEACHES / RECREATION AREAS

PLAYITA
(MANUEL ANTONIO NATIONAL PARK)

Popular nude beach inside Manuel Antonio National Park. Considered by some to be a gay nude beach. When you go, plan to stay a while because the beach can only be accessed at low tide. Once the tide has come in, you must wait until it goes back out before you can get in or out again.

> *DIRECTIONS:* Enter the park through the main entrance and park close to Playa Espadilla. Walk to the right as you face the ocean, wade across a stream and then walk across a cove. Climb over the rocks to reach Playita.

DENMARK

NUDE BEACHES / RECREATION AREAS

BELLEVUE STRAND
(NEAR COPENHAGEN)

Nude sunbathing occurs at the north end of this public beach. The extreme north end of the beach is the gay area.

DIRECTIONS: From Copenhagen go north along the coast about 7 kilometers and look for signs for Bellevue Strand. At the beach, walk to the left as you face the water to get to the north end.

FEDDET SYD-ØSTSTRAND
(NEAR FAKSE LADEPLADS)

Nude beach on the Feddet Peninsula, about 50 kilometers south of Copenhagen. The gay section is at the far end.

DIRECTIONS: Take Route E47/E55 south west from Copenhagen to the exit at junction 36. Go south on Route 151 to Longsted, then take Route 154 east toward Fakse, then south on Route 209 to Roholte and the camping area. Feddet Syd-Øststrand is beyond the beach called StrandeGård.

HVERRINGE SKOV STRAND
(FYN ISLAND)

The south end of this beach is particularly gay.

DIRECTIONS: From Kerteminde, head north past Nordstranden (the town's major beach) and take the first right after leaving town. At the sharp left curve turn right into the parking area.

HOVSTRUP STRAND
(NEAR ESBJERG)

This beach offers fantastic scenery off the North Sea. Popular with nudists, both gay and straight.

DIRECTIONS: From Esbjerg, go north to the town of Nørre Nebel and follow the signs.

TISVILDE STRAND — AKA TROLDESKOVEN STRAND
(NEAR COPENHAGEN)

The most popular nude beach in Denmark that has a distinct gay area.

DIRECTIONS: Take route A16 from Copenhagen to Frederiksværk, then northeast on Route 205 to Helsinge, then north on Route 237 to the turnoff to the west for Tisvildeleje. Parking is at Stranghus P-Plads. The nude area is southwest of the parking area.

FINLAND

NUDE BEACHES / RECREATION AREAS

PIHLAJASAARI
(OFF THE COAST OF HELSINKI)

Pihlajasaari refers to two islands off Helsinki's coast. The smaller of the two is used by nudists and is very popular with gay men.

> *DIRECTIONS:* Take the passenger ferry from Merisatama. Go left from the ferry dock and cross the footbridge to the smaller island.

RUISSALO SAARONNIEMI
(NEAR TURKU)

This island is connected to Turku by a bridge. The nude beach is on the far western end of the island.

> *DIRECTIONS:* The easiest way to get there is to take Bus 8 from The Market Square in Turku.

SEUSAARI
(NEAR HELSINKI)

This is a small island in an inlet near the center of Helsinki. Nude sunbathing occurs at the west end of the island. Walls separate male and female areas.

> *DIRECTIONS:* There is a footbridge that connects the island to the mainland. After crossing the bridge, the beach is to the right about one kilometer.

TURUN ULIMAHALLI
(NEAR TURU)

This is an indoor public pool and gym with certain days of the week being designated for men only. Nude swimming is common and exercising in the nude has also been seen here.

DIRECTIONS: Rehtorinpellontie 4 near Turku University and the main city hospital.

YYTERI BEACH
(NEAR PORI)

Located off the Gulf of Bothnia, this beach has a sanctioned nude area. The main clothed beach has many amenities.

DIRECTIONS: The best way to get there is to go to the Yyteri camping/resort area and have locals direct you to the nude area.

FRANCE

NUDE CLUBS / GROUPS / ORGANIZATIONS

CLAN NATURE (CLAN NATURE)

5, place de
l'Adjudant Vincenot
Paris 75020 France
(+33) 01 56 53 90 26
Email: contact@clannature.com
Website: www.clannature.com

CLOTHING-OPTIONAL ACCOMMODATIONS

LE LOFT

Chemin Haut Abrian
84100 Orange
France
(+33) 4 90 34 07 47 - Fax: (+33) 4 90 34 09 80
Email: hotel@homosphere.com

Guesthouse for gay men. 3 rooms, pool, gym, and lots of wooded areas. Nudity permitted at the pool.

NUDE BEACHES / RECREATION AREAS

BOUVERIE
(POITOU CHARENTES)

An Atlantic coast nude beach popular with gay men.

DIRECTIONS: From Saintes take Route N150 southwest about 40 kilometers to Royan, then go northwest on Route D25 about 30 kilometers. At the junction with Route D268 go left to the beach. The nude section is to the right as you are facing the water – about two kilometers up the beach.

CAP D'AGDE
(LANGUEDOC-ROUSSILLON)

If you are going to France, this is probably the place you should visit if you are a true nudist. Cap d'Agde is actually a naturist city. Here, nudity is REQUIRED on the beach and there have been patrols to make sure everybody is naked. When you're finished sunning, you can go to bars, the bank, stores, etc. all in the buff! Wear clothes to restaurants, however.

DIRECTIONS: Cap d'Agde is southwest of Montpellier and south of Agde. There are signs pointing to the nude quarter of the city. For information: Municipal du Tourisme et des Loisirs, BP 544, F-343305 Agde Cedex, France. Phone and fax: (+33) 6726 3858

FALAISE DES VACHES NOIRES
(AUBERVILLE)

The translation of the name of this beach is "Cliff of the Black Cows" and is reported to be popular with gay men.

DIRECTIONS: From Villers-sur-Mer, head west on Route D513 about 3 kilometers. Turn north onto Route D163, then look for a turnoff (immediate) to Auberville.

LOST-MARC'H
(BRETAGNE)

Located on the large peninsula south of Brest, northwest of Quimper. The peninsula branches out in three directions; the gay nude beach is located on the western shore of the southern branch.

DIRECTIONS: From Crozon take Route D887 south about one or one and a half kilometers. Just before the community of Morgat, the road will curve to the right and head west across the peninsula.

MARSEILLAN PLAGE
(LANGUEDOC-ROUSSILLON)

Very popular gay nude beach that gets very crowded in the summer.

DIRECTIONS: From Montpellier, take Route N112 southwest about 45 kilometers toward Sète and Agde to the small town of Marseillan Plage. Turn south to reach the main beach area in town, and then walk to the right to reach the nude area.

MIRAMAR
(AQUITAINE)

This beach is near the Spain/France border and is a popular gay nude beach.

DIRECTIONS: From Bayonne, go west to the neighboring town of Fiarritz. The beach is on the coastal road near the lighthouse (approximately a kilometer from the intersection of Route D910 and D911).

MONTALIVET
(AQUITAINE)

Montalivet Naturist Campground has a large beach. The gay section is on the south end where the nude beach expands off the campground property.

DIRECTIONS: From Bordeaux, go northwest on Route D215 about 65 kilometers to Lesparre-Médoc., then continue another 10 kilometers. Turn left onto Route D102 and continue about 8 kilometers to Montalivet-les-Bains. Head south of town to reach the beach.

PLAGE DE LA BATTERIE
(PROVENCE ALPES - CÔTE D'AZUR)

No sand on this beach, but large rocks for sunning. Very popular with gay men and can get cruisy at times.

DIRECTIONS: Take Route N7 east from Cannes. After a few kilometers, look for a gas station on the left side of the road (only structure there). There is a parking area near the gas station, also on the left. Use the train tunnel to cross under the road and reach the beach.

PLAGE DE ST-LAURENT D'EZE
(PROVENCE ALPES - CÔTE D'AZUR)

This beach has a reputation for being the gayest beach between St-Tropez and Monaco. It can get so crowded you can't lie on the beach without touching another person.

DIRECTIONS: From the port of Nice, take Basse Corniche (look for signs to this road) northeast approximately 20 kilometers toward Monaco. After passing through Eze-sur-Mer, you'll go through a tunnel. Just after the tunnel, turn left into the parking lot. Walk across the road and take the path to the beach.

ST-JEAN DES SABLES
(POITOU CHARENTES)

On the Atlantic coast of France and popular with gay men.

DIRECTIONS: From Rochelle go south on Route N137/E602 about 8 kilometers, then go west on Route D202. The beach is about one kilometer from the junction of those two roads.

VILLENEUVE-LÈS-MAGUELONE
(LANGUEDOC-ROUSSILLON)

One of the most popular gay nude beaches in France. There is often a rainbow flag marking the gay section where most people go nude.

DIRECTIONS: From Montpellier, go south on Route D986 several kilometers to the coastal town of Palavas-les-Flots. After the bridges, turn right at the sign pointing toward "Ifremer, Cathédrale de Maguilone." Continue to the parking lot (fee charged). When at the beach, walk right to the gay section. Island House for Men

GERMANY

CLOTHING-OPTIONAL ACCOMMODATIONS

HOTEL SONNENHOF

Ittling 36
91245 Simmelsdorf
Germany
(+49) 9155 7233
Fax: (+49) 9155 7278
Email: sonnenhof.hotel@t-online.de

Hotel for gay men. 20 rooms, one apartment. Nudity permitted in pool and at bar.

NUDE BEACHES / RECREATION AREAS

ANGERMUNDER BAGGERSEE (NEAR DÜSSELDORF)

A lake with a rocky beach for nude and clothed bathers. Very popular with local gay men.

DIRECTIONS: From Düsseldorf take Route A52 north toward Ratingen and Duisburg. Take the exit marked "Ratingen" (junction 23). Turn left at the first signal, then take a left at the next signal. You are now heading west (over Route A52) toward Kaiserswerth. Continue approximately one kilometer to the second parking area. There is a marked path to the north which you will need to hike on for about 10 minutes to reach the small lake. You can also take the S-bahn to the stop in Angermund just north of the lake.

GERMANY

BAGGERSEE SENDEN
(SENDEN)

Several lakes with designated clothing-optional areas. The far end of the third lake is where gay nudists can be found.

> *DIRECTIONS:* From Ulm take Route B19 to Senden. Go through the town and look for the sign to Baggersee Senden after you go through the south end of town. Park in the lot.

BÜRGERSEEN
(NEAR STUTTGART)

Small lake area with a popular gay nude site.

> *DIRECTIONS:* Take Route A8 (same as E52) southeast toward Ulm. Exit at junction 56 and go south on Route B297 toward Nürtingen for approximately one and a half kilometers. Turn left immediately after the gate. You can park down this road in a lot by the lake. The gay section is at the end of the second lake.

ENGLISCHER GARTEN
(MUNICH)

This is a city park that covers twice the area of Central Park. There are several clothing-optional areas within the park; the most popular area for gay men is Schönfeldwiese.

> *DIRECTIONS:* The park is a major landmark in Munich. Once there, you can reach the gay nude section by finding the southwest corner of the park. The field is inside an oval horseback riding track. This is near Haus der Kunst art museum on Prince Regent Street and is next to the Japanese Teahouse (east of the U-bahn station Universität).

EPPLE BAGGERSEE
(RHEINSTETTEN-FORCHHEIM)

A manmade lake with a designated clothing-optional area that is frequented by gay men.

> *DIRECTIONS:* Take Route B36 south from Karlsruhe toward the airport and look for signs for the lake in Rheinstetten-Forchheim.

FREIZEITGELÄNDE
(NEAR FRANKFURT)

A public pool facility with hot springs and baths. The nude crowd is mostly gay.

DIRECTIONS: Call (+49) 561 7822458 for directions.

HALLENBAD OST
(KASSEL)

A public pool with nude swimming on certain evenings. Gay men frequent the pool on nude evenings. Call for recent nude times.

DIRECTIONS: Located at Leipziger Strasse 99 in Kassel. Phone (+49) 561 7822458.

HEILIGER SEE
(POTSDAM)

This popular nude beach located in Neuer Garten attracts a mixed crowd that includes gay men as well as students from the nearby university.

DIRECTIONS: Take bus 116 from Berlin or tram 93 from Potsdam to Glienicker Brücke, and then go north to Neuer Garten.

KATZENBACHSEE
(BRACKENHEIM)

A lake beach that is nude on one side, clothed on the other. Local gay men frequent the nude side.

DIRECTIONS: Take the road to Brackenheim from southwest Heilbronn. Park at Katzenbachsee and go around the lake to the nude section.

KIRCHENTELLINSFURT BAGGERSEE
(NEAR STUTTGART)

A manmade lake whose nude beach is popular with gay men and can be cruisy.

DIRECTIONS: Take Route B27 south from Stuttgart toward Tübingen. Turn around at the Kirchentelinsfurt exit, and then take the Nürtingen exit. Shortly after taking this eastward turn, you will see signs for the lake. There is a fee charged. Go through the underpass, then left past the first lake. Follow the trail to the second lake. The gay section is at the far end.

KLEINER RIEDSEE
(PFOHREN)

Three lakes, one of which is designated for nude use. Near the borders of Switzerland and France. The nude lake is popular with local gay men.

DIRECTIONS: From Donaueschingen take Route B27 south to the Hüfingen exit, and then follow the signs toward Riedsee camping in Pfohren. Park there then walk through the woods to the lake.

LANGENER WALDSEE
(FRANKFURT)

A lake beach with a grassy lawn that has a designated nude section. Popular with gay men.

DIRECTIONS: From central Frankfurt, take Highway B44 southwest toward Mörfelden-Walldorf. Look for signs to Langener Waldsee, which is on the left side of B44. There are several small lakes in the park area has several lakes, the largest of which is Waldsee.

LEOPOLDSHAFENER BAGGERSEE
(NEAR LEOPOLDSHAFEN)

The clothing-optional section of this manmade lake is where the island is in view. Popular with gay men and can be cruisy.

DIRECTIONS: Take Route B36 north from Karlsruhe to the first parking lot for the lake after Leopoldshafen.

MIRAMAR FREIZEIT UND BADEZENTRUM
(WEINHEIM)

A public pool and sauna offering nude swimming on certain evenings. These evenings can be particularly gay.

DIRECTIONS: There are signs for Miramar off the freeway exits into town. Phone (+49) 6201-60000

STRANDBAD WANNSEE
(NEAR BERLIN)

This is a lake beach with a section sanctioned for nudity. It is located in Forst Grunewald Berlin's largest uninterrupted area of woods.

DIRECTIONS: Take S-bahn to Nikolassee station or bus 118 to Badweg, and then walk to the lake. In summer you can take bus 513 directly to the lake. The nude section is to the north on deck B.

SYLT

Sylt is an island off the North Sea coast of Germany. It boasts a lot of nude beaches (designated "FKK") and is a popular gay vacation destination. The most popular nude beach for gay men is the one near Westerland, the principal town on Sylt.

DIRECTIONS: Sylt is reached by taking a car train across a causeway. Inquire locally for directions to the train.

TEUFELSEE
(NEAR BERLIN)

This beach, like Strandbad Wannsee, is located in Forst Grunewald. It is not officially a nude beach, but nude bathers are well-tolerated and the beach is popular with gay men.

DIRECTIONS: Take the S-bahn (line S7) to Grunewald Station, or take bus 186 or 219. Teufelsee is about a half an hour walk west through the woods. The lake is at the edge of Teufelsberg, an attraction at Forst Grunewald.

SOMMERBAD KREUZBERG
(BERLIN)

A public pool that has a nude section of the lawn for sunbathing that is frequented by gay men. *DIRECTIONS:* Located at Gitschiner Strasse 18-31 in Berlin. Phone (+49) 3025 885412

STADTBAD CHARLOTTENBURG
(CHARLOTTENBURG)

A small public pool with nude swimming on certain days. Gay men frequent the pool at nude times. Call for the nude days.

DIRECTIONS: Located at Krumme Strasse 10 in Charlottenburg (Western Berlin). Phone: (+49) 3034 303214.

TUNTENWEISE — AKA TIERGARTEN (BERLIN)

The translation is "Queen's Meadow" – need we say more? A very gay sunbathing spot located in Tiergarten, a city park in the northeastern part of Berlin.

> *DIRECTIONS:* Take the S-bahn to get to Tiergarten. Go to the Victory Column, then face southeast. Between the two intersecting streets of Jofjägerallee and Strasse des 17.Juni just past the restrooms there is a path that leads to Tutenweise.

WELLENBAD AQUADROM (BAD URACH)

This public pool has designated nude swimming hours on Friday and Saturday nights. These hours attract gay men.

> *DIRECTIONS:* Located at Bei den Terman 8 in Bad Urach.
> Phone (+49) 7125 1666.

WOLFRATSHAUSEN (MUNICH)

Some 35 km south of Munich, this is the most popular site for gay men from the city. It is located at the confluence of the Isar and Loisach rivers, just north of the town of Wolfratshausen.

There are no facilities. The rivers come straight off the mountains, are swift and bracing, and very rocky – some sort of tightly-fitting footgear is advised. The dunes and woods are active. Parking will be a problem (except on Sundays) – easiest form of transportation is the S-Bahn line S7 to the end of the line (Wolfratshausen).

Walk north from the station on the footpath along the Loisach to the Weidacher Hauptstrasse (where a small steel bridge crosses the river) and walk east to the Isarspitz (street), then north following signs to the "Klaranlage" (water treatment plant). Where the street forms a Y, take the right branch; the trailhead is where the street dead ends at the plant. Proceed north, favoring the trails going off to the right when there's a choice, until you hit the dunes, then slightly northeast to the beach where most of the gay men gather.

> If traveling by car, find the Weidacher Hauptstrasse about 2 km north of the town center on the road from Wolfratshausen to Icking. On Sundays, park at the "Netto" supermarket; proceed across the Loisach on the small steel bridge and follow directions above.

GREECE

NUDE BEACHES / RECREATION AREAS

BANANA BEACH — AKA AMMOUDIA KRASSA (SKIATHOS)

There are actually two "Bananas" - there's "Big Banana" and "Little Banana"... and as surprising as it may seem for gay men, the one called "Little Banana" is where you'll find gay nudists! There is a taverna on the beach. This beach is also called "Banana Two" and "Spartacus Beach."

DIRECTIONS: From Skiathos town, take the 30-minute bus ride to Koukounaries (Golden Sand Beach). Take the track on the opposite side of the road from the bus stop. There are signs pointing to Banana Beach. Keep to the right at all turns as you climb a hill. At the top, go to the gate of a private villa, then turn left and descend the steep track. When the track forks, the right fork is for Little Banana; but it is suggested you go to Big Banana and then walk the beach to Little Banana. This hike takes about 15 minutes.

EFTALOU BEACH (LESBOS)

Located on the north coast of the island, this beach has a mixed crowd that includes gay men.

DIRECTIONS: From Molyvos, go east on the small coastal road that leads off from the school. After 5 kilometers, this road will become a dirt track. From this point there are nine bays; the seventh, eighth, and ninth bays are nude.

ELIA BEACH
(MYKONOS)

While this beach is growing in popularity, it is still a more secluded beach than Super Paradise. The western end is nude and predominantly male.

DIRECTIONS: The easiest way to get there is to take a bus from Mykonos town.

KOLOUMBO BEACH
(SANTORINI)

Santorini (Thira) is not known for its nude beaches, but this is one of them. It attracts a mixed crowd that includes gay men. You can't get there without transportation (no public transportation available).

DIRECTIONS: From the main road in Oia, take the paved road toward Baxedes. Follow the paved road until it turns to dirt, then go about 3 more kilometers to a parking area. Paths lead down the cliff, then a short walk away from the cliff that forms the south end of the beach.

MANTOMATA BEACH — AKA FALIRAKI BEACH
(RHODES)

The proprietors of this beach insist that you either be naked or be accompanied by someone who is naked. About half the crowd is gay.

DIRECTIONS: Find Hotel Danæ in Faliraki. About 50 meters beyond the hotel turn left onto a dirt road that goes uphill to a parking area. A short path leads to the nude beach. Also accessible by bus.

MYRTIOTISSA BEACH
(KÉRKYA)

This is said to be the most beautiful beach on the Mediterranean and attracts nude users from around the world. Many of the users are gay. The hike to get to it is rather strenuous, so the crowd tends to be younger.

DIRECTIONS: Take the beach access road in Vatos. The road is marked with a sign on a tree that says "To Myrtiotissa Beach." Your vehicle may be able to make it part way down the access road, but most will want to park on the main road. After walking down the access road, you will need to descend a cliff about 800 feet. The nude section is to the south. Accessible by bus from Corfu.

MONASTIRI BEACH
(PAROS)

This island is more peaceful than Mykonos and attracts a number of gay men.

DIRECTIONS: Take a fishing boat to the beach from the town of Naousa.

RAMNOUS BEACH
(ATHENS)

One of the few mainland nude beaches in Greece, this beach draws a significant gay crowd.

DIRECTIONS: Starting from Marathónas, take the highway with signs for Ramnous about 10 kilometers to the east, then turn left onto the paved road marked "Grammatiko." After approximately two and a half kilometers you'll come to a dirt road on the right at the fenced in ruins of the shrine of Ramnous. Turn right and navigate northward through a maze of dirt roads until you reach an old church near the beach. Park near the church and walk to the beach. The nude section is to the right.

ROMANOS BEACH
(PELOPONNESE)

This is not a tourist beach. It is visited mostly by local Greek men, and the dunes can be cruisy.

DIRECTIONS: From Pilos, take Route 9 north about 10 kilometers to the turnoff to the west for Romanos village. Once in the village, follow signs to the beach.

SUPER PARADISE BEACH
(MYKONOS)

A traditionally gay, nude beach on the island of Mykonos that is mostly rocks and pebbles, rather than sand. This beach is famous, so watch for gawking tourists (try nearby Elia Beach if they get too obnoxious). There is a taverna on the beach.

DIRECTIONS: Take a bus to Plati Yialos from Mykonos, and then take a fishing boat to the beach.

TSAMADOU BEACH
(SAMOS)

Tsamadou is very popular and draws a lot of tourists from Germany. The beach has a large attendance of gay men as well.

DIRECTIONS: Buses run from Samos town and the beach is marked with signs. From the bus stop, take the stairs to the beach and walk right to reach the nude area.

VAI BEACH
(CRETE)

Nude beach on the peninsula that stretches northward into the sea. The nude section is smaller and attracts gay men.

DIRECTIONS: Follow signs to the main beach in Vai. Take the wooden walkway to the right as you face the water. Pass a taverna, and then go uphill and over the headland to reach a smaller beach. There are other nude beaches on Crete as well.

ICELAND

CLOTHING-OPTIONAL ACCOMMODATIONS

ROOM WITH A VIEW

Laugavegur 18, 6th floor
Reykjavík 101
Iceland
(+354) 552-7362
Fax: (+354) 552-7262
Email: info@roomwithaview.is
Website: www.roomwithaview.is

Apartments mostly for gay men. 6 apartments. Hot tub, pools, saunas, gyms in town. No restrictions on nudity.

INDONESIA

CLOTHING-OPTIONAL ACCOMMODATIONS

PURI WIMPY BALI VILLA

Jalan Kayu Aya 15A
Bsangkasa, Kuta, Bali 80361
Indonesia
(+62) (0) (361) 730326
Mobile: (+62) (0) 8123868628
Email: puriwimpy@yahoo.com
Website: www.puriwimpy.com

Guesthouse for gay men. 4 rooms. Clothing optional in pool area if renting entire house. If renting a single room, nudity in the pool is subject to comfort level of other guests.

IRELAND

CLOTHING-OPTIONAL ACCOMMODATIONS

FAIRFIELD LODGE

Monkstown Avenue
Monkstown, Co. Dublin
Ireland
(+353) 1 2803912
Fax: (+353) 1 2803912
Email: jsb@indigo.ie
Website:
www.inntravels.com/ireland/rdfairfield.html

A studio apartment for gay men. Close to gay bars in Dublin. Nudity permitted in private garden area.

NUDE BEACHES / RECREATION AREAS

FORTY FOOT (DUBLIN)

A traditional nude beach that was used exclusively by men. As with Kilkee Beach, these areas were designated nude because they didn't allow women or had separate areas for women to bathe nude. Lately, women have started to use Forty Foot, but it remains used mostly by men. This beach is popular with gay men, but discretion is important because of its traditional men-only status. There are many straight men here as well, including some that are more "conservative" in their views.

> *DIRECTIONS:* Coming south from Dublin to Dun Laoghaire on the road that runs near the coast, look for signs for Forty Foot just before Martello Tower. Also accessible by Dublin Area Rapid Transport.

IRELAND

KILKEE BEACH
(COUNTY CLARE)

This is a quiet beach with traditional nude use - almost exclusively by men.

DIRECTIONS: From Limerick, take Route N18 north to Ennis, then Route N68 west to Kilrush, then follow the signs northwest several miles to the town of Kilkee on the coast. Access the beach from the town, and then walk right toward the cliffs to get to the nude section.

ISRAEL

NUDE BEACHES / RECREATION AREAS

**GA'ASH BEACH
(TEL AVIV)**

This beach is popular with gay men and gets most crowded on Fridays and Saturdays.

> *DIRECTIONS:* From Tel Aviv go north on the coastal highway toward Haifa for about 24 kilometers. When you reach the small sign that marks the entrance to the Ga'ash Kibbuts, turn left. After about 100 yards, turn right onto a dirt road Follow the main dirt road and turn left to the large parking lot on a cliff overlooking the beach. Climb down to the beach at the south end of the parking lot.

ITALY

NUDE BEACHES / RECREATION AREAS

CAPOCOTTA AND TOR VAIÁNICA BEACHES
(IL BUCO, ROME)

Of these two nude beaches in Rome, Capocotta is frequented by more gay men. Both are popular nude sites.

DIRECTIONS: Take Via Cristoforo Colombo southwest from Rome to the end of the route at the coast then go south on Route S601. Continue south and look for kilometer marker 7. The entrance to Capocotta is between marker 7 and 8. You may have to walk a bit to the beach entrance depending on how many cars are parked.

CAPRI

A rocky beach on the south side of the island has a nude beach that is popular with gay men.

DIRECTIONS: Take Via Krupp south from the town of Capri to where it is closed. Walk around the barricade to reach the beach just below it.

LETOJANNI
(SICILY)

A nude beach with a mixed crowd located in Taormina.

DIRECTIONS: From Taormina head north on S114 to Letojanni. Continue north and watch for a sign that says "Camping Paradise." About one half kilometer past the sign there is a parking area. A path leads through a tunnel under the railroad tracks to the beach.

LIDO DEGLI ALBERONI
(VENICE)

A predominantly gay nude beach often called simply "The Lido."

DIRECTIONS: The easiest way to get here is via water bus. Take bus B for the village of Alberoni. The nude beach is near the lighthouse.

LIDO DI DANTE AND LIDO DI CLASSE
(RAVENNA)

These two beaches are close to each other and both are popular gay nude sites. LIDO DI CLASSE is the more popular of the two.

DIRECTIONS: Go south from Ravenna on Route SS16 to Sávio, and then look for the road on the left side of the road that goes to Lido di Classe. The nude beach is to the north, getting more gay the farther north you go (left as you face the water).

PIEVE LIGURE
(GENOA)

A remote beach that is predominantly gay.

DIRECTIONS: From Genoa, take Route S1 east about 10-15 kilometers to the Pieve Ligure railway station. The nude beach is about 100 meters from the station. Head left when facing the water to reach the gay area.

PONTE DI VIDOR
(VENICE)

A river beach that is very popular with gay nudists.

DIRECTIONS: From Treviso take Route S13 north to the Piave River. After crossing the river, turn left on the road that parallels the north bank of the river (toward Colfosco). After approximately twenty kilometers you will reach Vidor. Continue west a few kilometers until you see a bridge on the left that crosses the Piave River. Continue past the bridge (do not take the bridge) and then make the first left. Go toward the river to park. Walk to the river.

ROCCA DI MANERBA
(NEAR VERONA)

This nudist site is popular with gay men and is located on the southwestern shores of Lago di Garda.

DIRECTIONS: Take Route A4 about 40 kilometers west from Verona. Take the turnoff for the town of Desenzano del Garda. From Desenzano del Garda, head north on Route S572 for 8-10 kilometers, then turn right on the turnoff to Moniga del Garda. Follow the signs to "Parco Naturale" and park. Take the footpath Via Marinello for about 15 minutes. Look for the huge natural rock formation to find the nude beach.

SAN SABA
(SICILY)

Nude beach on Sicily. Look for the gay section after you get to the beach.

DIRECTIONS: From Messina take Route A20 or S113 west to the village of Divieto. From Diviento head northeast on the coastal road S113d to San Saba.

SAN VIGILIO BEACH
(NEAR VERONA)

Another nude beach on Lago di Garda that has a mixed crowd with many gay men.

DIRECTIONS: From Verona take Route S11 west about 23 kilometers to Peschiera del Garda, then go right onto Route S249 and continue about 18 kilometers to the village of Garda. Continue past Garda on S249. When the road turns sharply to the right, look for the beach access.

SARDINIA
(CAGLIARI)

There are several nude beaches on Sardinia, but the ones preferred by gay men are located here. The one in Cala Mosca is often called "Cala Gay" by locals. The other beach, Terra Mala, attracts a younger crowd.

DIRECTIONS: Take the coastal road east form Cagliari to the turnoff for Cala Mosca. On the beach, walk toward the San Elia lighthouse to find the nude area. Farther east is Terra Mala.

SISTIANA
(TRIESTE)

A nude beach near the Croatian border with a mixed crowd that includes gay men.

> *DIRECTIONS:* From Trieste go north on S14 to the village of Sistiana. Look for a bar named Dosta dei Barbari. The path to the beach is across form the bar and parking is nearby. Once at the beach, walk to the left for about ten minutes to reach the nude section.

SPERLONGA
(NEAR ROME)

This beach between Rome and Naples is popular with all kinds of people - including gay men. Officials don't like it when you remain nude in their presence, so keep a cover handy.

> *DIRECTIONS:* From Rome take Route S7 south about 100 kilometers to Terracina. Just past Terracina, take Route S213 south along the coast about 15-20 kilometers to Sperlonga. Look for signs to Sperlonga Park. Go to the park and walk toward the Grotto. The nude beach is about 100 meters from the Grotto.

TALVERA RIVER
(BOLZANO)

A riverbank nude beach that is attended mostly by gay men.

> *DIRECTIONS:* From Bolzano (Bozen) head north on Route S508 (toward Pnticino and Sarentino). Just north of Bolzano, look for a turnoff at a sign that says "Bar Seeberger Jausestation." Turn here and take the road to the end, then walk bout 500 meters along the river to the nude area.

TORBOLE
(NEAR VERONA)

This is a third site on Lago di Garda frequented by gay men.

> *DIRECTIONS:* From Verona take Route A22 north about 60 kilometers. Just south of Roverto, turn west onto Route S240. Continue about 15-20 kilometers to the town of Torbole. In Torbole, turn left onto Route S249. Within a kilometer or so you will cometo a tunnel. Park near the tunnel and go down to the water.

RIVER TICINO
(MILAN)

This is Milan's unofficial nude beach that is not exclusively gay, but popular with local gay men.

DIRECTIONS: From Milan take Route S494 west toward Vigévano. Just before reaching Vigévano you will come to a bridge over the Ticino River. Park just before the bridge. Walk to the river, either through the main park gate or through wooded trails near the highway. At the river, turn left and walk about 2 kilometers. The area with the sandbars is the nude section.

MEXICO

NUDE CLUBS / GROUPS / ORGANIZATIONS

G-NATURA (G-N)

APDO Postal 21-002
C.P. 04021
Mexico, D.F. Mexico
Email: gnaturag@yahoo.com
Since March 2000

Approx: 80 members
Potential members welcome
Monthly social activities, outdoors, and camping trips in Mexico.

CLOTHING-OPTIONAL ACCOMMODATIONS

ACAPULCO CASA DEL MAR

Calle La Bocana 12-18
Fracc. Las Playas
Acapulco, Buerrero
Mexico 39390
(+52) 7 482 16 36
Email: aca@aca.cableonline.com.mx

A guesthouse for gay men. 5 rooms. Nudity permitted in pool and terrace areas.

ACAPULCO LAS PALMAS

155 Ave Las Conchas
Fracto, Farallon C.P. 39690
Acapulco
Mexico
(+52) 7 444 {87 0843}
Fax: (+52) 7 444 {87 1282}
Email: bobbyjoe@acapulco-laspalmas.com
Website: www.acapulco-laspalmas.com

Clothing-optional resort located in Acapulco for gay men and gay women. Private baths, TV, VCR, Jacuzzi/pool.

ARCO IRIS

#115 Paseo de los Delfines
Fracc. Conchas Chinas
Puerto Vallarta, Jalisco C.P. 48390
Mexico
(+52) 322 15579
Fax: (+52) 322 15586

Bed and breakfast for gay men and lesbians. 17 rooms (9 with private baths), 5 suites, 2 apartments, 4 casitas (3- or 4- bedrooms and private pool). Nudity permitted throughout, except upper gate and upper terrace.

VALLARTA CORA

Calle Pilitas #174
Colonia Emiliano Zapatas
Puerto Vallarta, Jalisco 48380
Mexico from US: (888) 869-9301
(+52) 322 222-6234
Fax: (+52) 322 32815 EXT 104
Email: info@vallartacora.com
Website: www.vallartacora.com/

Hotel mostly for gay men. 14 units, all with kitchens. Heated pool with poolside bar. Clothing-optional around the pool.

NUDE BEACHES / RECREATION AREAS

CABAÑAS DON ARMANDOS (TULUM)

This is an area of rental cabins on the beach near Tulum, which is best known for its Mayan ruins. The clientele is mixed and it is a good idea to cover up if the police should happen to patrol; staying naked in their presence could upset them.

DIRECTIONS: If there is not a sign on Highway 307, ask in Tulum where Cabañas Don Armandos is. The rates for the cabins are extremely reasonable.

PLAYA DEL CARMEN (YUCATAN PENINSULA)

An unofficial nude beach near the Shangri-La Hotel with white sand and turquoise water. The dunes can be cruisy.

DIRECTIONS: From the beach at the Shangri-La Hotel on the north end of town, walk north (left facing the water) about 100 yards past the palapa bar to the nude section.

PLAYA ZIPOLITE (OAXACA)

An unofficial nude beach in an undeveloped section of Mexico's southern Pacific coast. Tourists from Europe, Australia and the US use the beach with some of the users being gay men. There are guesthouses and a couple restaurants nearby. Camping is permitted on the beach.

DIRECTIONS: Drive to Puerto Angel (the end of Highway 175 - about 250 kilometers south of Oaxaca). Playa Zipolite is 4 kilometers west of Puerto Angel. You can take a taxi to the beach if you wish.

NETHERLANDS

NUDE CLUBS / GROUPS / ORGANIZATIONS

NAKED CLUB AMSTERDAM (NC ADAM)
C/O HENNY HOLLA

Warmoes Str. 93
1012 H.Z. Amsterdam, HOLLAND

1 party per month

NUDE BEACHES / RECREATION AREAS

HOEK VAN HOLLAND
(DEN HAAG)

This is a port town in southern Holland with a small, officially nude beach that can be cruisy at times for gay men.

DIRECTIONS: The nude beach has signs in Hoek van Holland and is accessible by train.

ZANDVOORT BEACH
(NEAR AMSTERDAM)

The most popular nude beach in the Netherlands, Zandvoort Beach has all the amenities: vendors, food, lifeguards, showers, restrooms, and chair rentals. There is a specific gay area.

DIRECTIONS: The best way to get to the beach at Zandvoort is to take the train from Amsterdam's Centraal Station. There are trains for the beach every half hour during the summer and the ride is about 40 minutes. Once at the train station in Zandvoort, the nude beach is south. Walk for about 40 minutes south (left facing the water) to reach the gay section. Cabs are available if you don't want to walk.

NEW ZEALAND

NUDE CLUBS / GROUPS / ORGANIZATIONS

AUCKLAND SUNBOYS

PO Box 4478
Shortland St
Auckland, New Zealand
Phone: +64-9-418-2388
Email: aklsunboys@hotmail.com
Website: www.gaynz.net.nz/sunboys/about.htm

The club has 2 get-togethers per month. In the summer they are generally pool days or visits to nude beaches. In the winter they are monthly nude hot pools night, nude dinners, nude bar nights and introduction to massage. Visitors welcome. Dues: NZ$10. No newsletter – event reminders are emailed.

CLOTHING-OPTIONAL ACCOMMODATIONS

AUTUMN FARM

R.D. 1 Takaka
Golden Bay, Nelson 7172
New Zealand
(+64) 3 525-9013
Fax: (+64) 3 525 7122
Email: stay@autumnfarm.com
Website: www.autumnfarm.com

Guesthouse, camping and backpacker accommodation for men. Open all year. Comfortable colonial home with communal bath-house, kitchen and laundry facilities on 12 acres of gardens, fields and woodlands. Close to rivers, beaches and National Parks. Clothing optional throughout. Summer Camp over New Year period and Naked Week Festival Feb 7-15, annually. New Zealand's premier gay nudist resort.

CORNUCOPIA LODGE

361-363 State Highway 5
R.D. 2 Eskdale
Napier, Hawke's Bay
New Zealand
(+64) 6 836 6508
Fax: (+64) 6 836 6518
Email: stay@cornucopia-lodge.com
Website: www.cornucopia-lodge.com

Bed and breakfast for anyone (the members of your party are the only guests). 2 bedroom cottage. Pool and grass tennis court. Nudity permitted throughout.

FRESH EGG RETREAT

Bute Road, R.D. 9
Tinui, Masterton 5921
New Zealand
(+64) 6 372 3506
Fax: (+64) 6 372 3505
Email: freshegg@hotmail.com

Bed and breakfast retreat for gay men, lesbians, and straight people. 2 rooms. Pool, sauna, gym. Nudity permitted throughout (confirm in advance).

OCEAN VIEW HEIGHTS

125 Ocean View Road
Northcote, Auckland 1309
New Zealand
(+64) 9 418 2388
Fax: (+64) 9 480 3155
Email: oceanview@xtra.co.nz

Bed and breakfast for gay men. 2 rooms. Pool, hot tub, private garden. Nudity permitted poolside (and inside according to comfort level of guests).

NEW ZEALAND

NUDE BEACHES / RECREATION AREAS

BREAKER BAY
(NEAR WELLINGTON)

An officially clothing-optional beach that has a gay following.

DIRECTIONS: From the end of State Route 1 in Wellington, follow the sign toward the airport. Turn right at the second roundabout continuing toward the airport. Turn left onto Broadway toward Strathmore and Seatoun continue through Strathmore and the tunnel. Take the first right after the tunnel onto Ludlam Street, then turn right onto Inglis Street. Continue through the Pass of Branda to the two parking lots on the left after driving down a hill. Walk to the beach. The nude section is past the rock arch.

PAPAMOA BEACH
(TAURANGA)

There is some question as to whether this beach is officially nude, but traditionally it has been used that way and attracts many gay men.

DIRECTIONS: From Tauranga, follow the signs toward Mount Maunganui. Just past the railroad crossing, turn right at the roundabout onto Girven Road. Turn right at Maranui Road at the sign to Papamoa. Continue for 2 kilometers past the Bay Park Raceway and park near the Papamoa Beach sign. Walk left as you face the water to reach the nude beach.

PEKA PEKA BEACH
(NEAR WELLINGTON)

An undeveloped beach that is frequented by gay men.

DIRECTIONS: From Wellington go north on State Route 1 about 65 kilometers to Waikanae. Continue north about five more kilometers, then turn left onto Te Haupa Road. Park at the end and take the trail to the beach. The nude area is south (left as you face the water).

POHUTUKAWA BEACH
(NEAR AUCKLAND)

This beach is less accessible during high tide. During that time you must walk on a cliff top path. Popular with gay men.

DIRECTIONS: Go north from Auckland about 30 kilometers on the Northern Motorway. Look for Rosedale Road and turn right, then turn left onto east Coast Bays Road and continue for 3 kilometers. Turn right onto Carlisle Road and continue to the ARA reserve at the end of the road. Drive through the reserve and park in the northernmost lot. Walk to the left as you face the water for about 30 minutes. The beach is around an outcropping of rock. Long Bay Bus 839 from Auckland also stops near the beach.

SPENCERVILLE BEACH
(CHRISTCHURCH)

Most of the beaches on the south Island can be nude; this one is established and enjoys use by many gay men.

DIRECTIONS: From Christchurch, go north on Marshlands Road. Turn right onto Lower Styx Road at the sign to Spencerville. As you approach the coast, stay left on the bumpy road through the trees and park at the end. Walk to the left to reach the nude section of the beach.

ST. LEONARD'S BEACH
(NEAR TAKAPUNA)

This beach is not far from Auckland and draws many gay men.

DIRECTIONS: From Takapuna, go south on Lake Road approximately two kilometers, then turn left onto St. Leonard's Road. Beach parking is at the end of this road. Take the stairs to the beach then walk left to the nude area.

URETITI BEACH
(WHANGAREI)

This is a well-known nude beach used mostly by men, some of them gay.

DIRECTIONS: From State Route 1, continue 6 kilometers north of Waipu. Turn right onto Uretiti Road and park at the beach. Walk to the right to reach the nude area.

NORWAY

NUDE CLUBS / GROUPS / ORGANIZATIONS

OSLO GAY NATURIST (OGN)
C/O AASMUND VIC

Falsens GATE 27-B
0556 Oslo, Norway
Email: rainbow360@czi.net

NUDE BEACHES / RECREATION AREAS

HUK BEACH
(NEAR OSLO)

Clothed and nude zones are separated by a small bay. There is a snack shop on the nude beach and a shower facility. The beach is very popular with gay men.

DIRECTIONS: Take bus 30 (Bygdøy) from downtown Oslo to the last stop. Continue down the road on foot to the parking lot at Huk. A path on the right side of the lot leads to the beach.

LANGØYENE ISLAND
(NEAR OSLO)

The southeastern part of the island is clothing-optional and a popular gay nude beach.

DIRECTIONS: Take passenger ferry no. 94 from the island of Vippetangen. Bus 60 from downtown Oslo goes to Vippetangen.

SILDEVIKA
(PORSGUNN)

Nudity on this beach is common and can also be found in the forested hill behind it. A popular site for gay men.

> *DIRECTIONS:* From Olavsberget Camping take Route E18. About 10 kilometers down the road there is a parking area on the right. Walk west past the road barrier. When the road narrows, there is a path to the right that leads to the beach.

SVARTKULP
(NEAR OSLO)

This is a small forest lake area with a nude beach popular for gay men.

> *DIRECTIONS:* Ask for directions to Sognsvann (a larger lake). Svartkulp is east of Sognsvann.

PORTUGAL

CLOTHING-OPTIONAL ACCOMMODATIONS

CASA MARHABA

Rua de Benagil, Alfanzina
8400-427 Lagoa
Algarve
Portugal
(+351) 282 358720
Fax: (+351) 282 358720
Email: tony@casamarhaba.com
Website: www.casamarhaba.com

A guesthouse for gay men. 5 rooms (all with private baths). Pool, sundeck, waterfall, barbecue. Nudity permitted in pool and on sundeck. Breakfast included.

NUDE BEACHES / RECREATION AREAS

PRAIA DE AIVADOS
(NEAR VILA NOVA DE MILFONTES)

A little-known unofficial nude beach with a gay following. This beach has natural springs.

DIRECTIONS: This beach is difficult to find due to the number of unmarked roads. It's best to ask locals how to get to Praia do Malhão (a clothed beach). Once on the beach, walk to the right as you face the water. Go over a small hill to the next beach.

PRAIA DA BELA VISTA
(NEAR LISBON)

Beach #17 is the most popular for gay use and tends to be cruisy. If you're not looking for the cruisy atmosphere, go to Praia do Meco, which is close by. As always, use your discretion – there have been reports of attacks on men cruising the dunes.

> *DIRECTIONS:* From Costa da Caparica take the road toward Fonte da Telha. The beach is about 7 kilometers south of Costa da Caparica. There is a bus from Lisbon to Costa da Caparica and a train that runs along the beach in summer that will take you to Beach #17.

PRAIA DA ILHA DE TAVIRA
(NEAR TAVIRA)

This officially nude beach is on a small barrier island and is a popular place to sunbathe for gay men.nude beach.

PRAIA DO GUINCHO
(NEAR LISBON)

This is not a nude beach, but it is very common for gay men to sunbathe nude in the dunes and it can get rather cruisy.

> *DIRECTIONS:* From Lisbon take Route N6 or Route A5 west to Cascais. There are signs in Cascais pointing to Praia do Guincho.

PRAIA DO MECO
(NEAR SESIMBRA)

This is the most popular nude beach in Portugal and draws all kinds of people, including gay men.

> *DIRECTIONS:* Take Route A2 south from Lisbon for fifteen kilometers, then exit and go south on Route N378 toward Sesimbra. In Marco do Grilo, turn right on the road that goes to Lagoa de Albufeira and Alfarim. Continue to Alfarim and turn right at the primary school. This road leads to Aldeia do Meco, where you will bear right onto a rough road that leads two kilometers to beach perking. The nude beach is to the left as you face the water. More gay men tend to gather farther south.

PRAIA DA PONTA DA PIEDADE
(NEAR LAGOS)

A popular, though not official, nude beach. It is a cove beneath cliffs and is popular with gay men.

DIRECTIONS: Lagos is at the junction of Routes N120 and N125 in southwestern Portugal. The nude beach is at the lighthouse west of Praia do Camilo, south of Lagos.

VALE DO LOBO
(BETWEEN VALE DO LOBO AND QUARTEIRA)

An unofficial nude beach that is popular with gay men.

DIRECTIONS: From Faro take Route N125 about 15 kilometers to the turnoff for Vale do Lobo in Almancil. Parking is east of Vale do Lobo, near the restaurants at Quinta do Lago. Once at the beach, walk left as you face the water to reach the nude section.

RUSSIA

NUDE BEACHES / RECREATION AREAS

SEREBRYANYJ BOR — AKA SILVER PINE PARK (MOSCOW)

This park is in the northwestern part of Moscow. The nude beach is on a loop of the Moscow River. Many gay men sunbathe nude here. Clothing-optional status is legal here.

> *DIRECTIONS:* From the Metro Polezhaevskaia station in western Moscow, take tram 20 or 65. Both these lines make stops near the park. Once getting off the tram, walk left past a bar then right past a playground. Continue over two bridges then bear right through a grove of pine trees for about 650 feet to the beach.

SESTRORECK (NEAR ST. PETERSBURG)

A very social and popular nude beach. Here you can play badminton or volleyball or enjoy food from the vendors that are sometimes present. It is a popular place for gay naturists.

> *DIRECTIONS:* Take the Sestroreck Line on the commuter train from St. Petersburg's Finland Station. Get off at Kurort Station in Sestroreck and walk through Kurort Park. There is a footbridge on the eastern end of the park (right from the station). Cross the bridge and walk through the woods.

TEATRALUJU (SOCHI)

Sochi is a popular resort town and the nude beach here draws a few gay men.

SOUTH AFRICA

CLOTHING-OPTIONAL ACCOMMODATIONS

AMSTERDAM GUESTHOUSE

19 Forest Road, Oranjezicht
Cape Town 8001
South Africa
(+27) 21 461-8236
Fax: (+27) 21 461-5575
Email: info@amsterdam.co.za
Website: www.amsterdam.co.za

A guesthouse for gay men. 9 rooms (8 with private baths). Pool, hot tub, sauna, steam, gym, and sling room. Nudity permitted in pool area, wet areas, and the back yard. Breakfast included.

GREENMAN COTTAGE BED & BREAKFAST

1 Keerom Street
Barrydale, Klein Karoo 6750
South Africa
(+27) 28 572-1685
(+27) 83 311-1122 (mobile)
Fax: (+27) 28 572-1685
Email: greenman@ananzi.co.za

Bed and breakfast for gay men. 3 rooms with private baths. Near lake. Nudity permitted at the lake and indoors. All meals included.

NEWLANDS GUESTHOUSE

4 Alcis Road, Newlands
Cape Town 7700
South Africa
(+27) 21 686-0013
Fax: (+27) 21 686-9216
Cell: (083) 251-7274
Email: garth@newlandsguest.co.za
Website: www.newlandsguest.co.za

Bed and Breakfast for gay men and straight clientele. 5 rooms, one suite. Rooms are en suite (sitting room and bath). Nudity permitted at the pool. Breakfast included.

VOËLKOP FARM

Silver Jackals, Makolokwe
North West Province
South Africa
Mailing address: c/o Out in Africa Tours
P.O. Box 2431
Cresta 2118
South Africa
Farm: (+27) 12-2541157
Cell: (082) 880-7497
Email: voelkop@mweb.co.za
Website: www.voelkop.com

Resort and campground for gay men. Pools. No restrictions on nudity.

SOUTH AFRICA

NUDE BEACHES / RECREATION AREAS

GRAAFF'S POOL BEACH
(CAPE TOWN)

A men-only nude beach since the late 1800's (when swimming was segregated by gender). Gay men are beginning to use this beach.

DIRECTIONS: In Cape Town, the beach is across the street from the Winchester Mansions Hotel on Sea Front Road.

SANDY BAY
(CAPE TOWN)

This is the most popular nude beach in South Africa. The mountains join the water, creating fantastic scenery. The south end of Main Beach is the main gathering place for gay men.

DIRECTIONS: Take Victoria Drive from the Bakoven area and go south 5 kilometers past the Cape Town city limits. Turn right onto Llandudno Road which will become Fisherman's Bend. At the end of the road, turn right onto Sandy Bay Road and follow signs to the parking lot. A path will take you to Family Beach. Beyond Family Beach are enormous rocks, behind them is the bay and Main Beach.

UMHLANGA LAGOON
(DURBAN)

This is not a nude beach but is used by nudists without any hassle. Gay men can be found here.

DIRECTIONS: From Durban take the freeway M4 north to Umhlanga Rocks and follow the signs to the Umhlanga Lagoon Nature Reserve. The reserve is on the south bank of the Umhlanga River and just past the Breakers Hotel. Park on the street or in the lot. Walk through the preserve on the path that leads to the lagoon. The dunes tend to be the nude section.

SPAIN

CLOTHING-OPTIONAL ACCOMMODATIONS

CASA ALEXIO

Barrio Ses Torres 16
07819 Jesus - Talamanca
Ibiza
Spain
(+34) 971 31 42 49
Fax: (+35) 971 31 26 19
(800) 257-5344 (reserve through Odysseus)
(516) 944-5344 (outside US and Canada)
Email: alexio@alexio.com
Website: www.alexio.com

Guesthouse for gay men. 15 rooms. Pool, whirlpool, beach nearby. Nudity permitted anywhere, no restrictions.

FINCA LERÍA

Partido 'Los Anealés'
29500 Álora, Malaga
Spain
(+0034) 952-495-554
Fax: (+0034) 952-495-554
Website: www.fincaleriaguesthouse.com

A guesthouse mostly for gay men. 4 rooms (2 with private baths). Pool. Nudity permitted anywhere except during dinner. Meals included.

PASSION TROPICAL

Calle las Adelfas 6, An Augustin
35130 Playa del Ingles, Gran Canaria
Spain
(+34) 928 770131
Fax: (+34) 928 773771
(800) 257-5344
(reservations through Odysseus)
(516) 944-5330
(reservations through Odysseus outside US
and Canada)
Email: info@pasion-tropical.com
Website: www.pasion-tropical.com

Resort for gay men and lesbians. 15 villas, each with 2 bedrooms. Pool, hot tub, garden, gym. Nudity permitted anywhere.

VILLAS BLANCAS - 1

Avenida Tjaereborg
Campo de Golf
Maspalomas, Gran Canaria 35100
Spain
(+34) 902 168 169
(800) 257-5344
(reserve through Odysseus)
(516) 944-5344 (outside US and Canada)
Fax: (+34) 902 268 269
Email: vb@boesweb.com
Website: www.villasblancas.com

Resort with 24 bungalows for gay men. Pool, gym, sauna nearby. Nudity permitted in pool area. Newly remodeled.

VILLAS BLANCAS - 2

Avenida Tjaereborg
Campo de Golf
Maspalomas, Gran Canaria 35100
Spain
(+34) 902 168 169
(800) 257-5344 (reserve through Odysseus)
(516) 944-5344 (outside US and Canada)
Fax: (+34) 902 268 269
Email: vb@boesweb.com
Website: www.villasblancas.com

Gay men only. Six 2 or 3 bedroom villas and a second pool.

VILLA MAREU

Calle Matkatala 18A
Campo de Golf
Maspalomas, Gran Canaria
SPAIN
(+34) 928 77 42 35
Fax: (+34) 928 77 42 35
Email: nicholas.lpa@idecnet.com

Private villa (must book entire villa). 2 bedrooms and 2 baths. Pool, gym. Sauna nearby. Nudity permitted anywhere.

NUDE BEACHES / RECREATION AREAS

AZKORRI HONDARTZA (BASQUE COUNTRY)

This beach is friendly with a mixed crowd. About half the people go nude but the end of the beach sees much more nude use.

DIRECTIONS: From Gexto follow the signs to Azkorri Hondartza (hondartza is Basque for "beach").

CABO PINO (MARBELLA)

The most popular nude beach in the Costa del Sol region, this beach is very popular with gay men. It is very cruisy and even has a beach bar where clothing is not required.

DIRECTIONS: From Mirabella go east on Route N340. After about 10 kilometers, look for Hotel Arola, and then look for kilometer marker 194. Just past the marker take the first right (road may not be marked). Take the third left, go to the end, park, and walk over the dunes to the beach. You can take a bus to Hotel Arola and walk to the beach, if you wish.

CALA DE BOADELLA (COSTA BRAVA)

This is a small nude beach that can get very crowded. Popular with gay men and can get cruisy at times.

DIRECTIONS: The beach is near Hotel Santa Cristina. There is a McDonald's near the beach. Ask for directions locally.

ES CAVALLET
(IBIZA)

The island of Ibiza has an established gay tourist scene. The beach draws almost exclusively gay men and is almost completely nude. It also has amenities such as restrooms, a bar, snack vending, and beach umbrella rentals.

DIRECTIONS: From Ibiza town follow the signs to the airport on Route PM801. Just past Sant Jordi, turn left onto PM802 toward Sa Canal. About 4 kilometers down the road is the turnoff for the beach (there is a sign). The beach is also accessible by bus (take the bus to Playa de Ses Salines, which is adjacent to Es Cavallet).

PLATJA DEL SALER
(NEAR VALENCIA)

A nude beach that is used by a number of gay men.

DIRECTIONS: From Valencia, take Route CV500 south along the coast for about 15 kilometers. Look for the sign. The nude section is to the right when facing the water.

PLAYA BENALNATURA
(TORREMOLINOS)

Málaga and Torremolinos are hard to separate, but Torremolinos is much more gay. The nude beach has many amenities with gay men gathering to the west (right) side of the beach.

DIRECTIONS: From Torremolinos go southwest along the coast to Benalmádena. The beach is near Casino Torrequebrada.

PLAYA DE CHERNOBYL
(NEAR BARCELONA)

Chernobyl is a nickname for this beach, so named because it is in the Badalona industrial area and the water is also quite polluted. But it is a very popular nude beach with gay men and can be cruisy.

DIRECTIONS: Take Metro Line 4 to Sant Roc Station. The beach is east about one kilometer.

PLAYA GUASIMETA
(CANARY ISLANDS)

A nude beach on the island of Lanzarote. Popular with gay men and can be cruisy.

DIRECTIONS: Coming east from Puerto del Carmen, look for signs for Playa Guasimeta past Playa de los Pocillos as you approach the airport. You can also look for signs for Punta Montañosa (same general area).

PLAYA DEL MAGO
(MALLORCA)

This beach, in addition to the gay-popular Es Trenc beach, is another choice for gay naturists on Mallorca. It is officially clothing-optional and is closer to the town of La Palma.

DIRECTIONS: From La Palma take the freeway southwest toward Peguera and Andratx. After approximately fifteen kilometers, go left toward Portals Vells and Cala Figuera. At the second intersection a sign points the way to Playa del Mago.

PLAYA DE MASPALOMAS
(CANARY ISLANDS)

An extremely popular, officially nude beach that can literally draw thousands of nude bathers. Gay men tend to gather on the east end of the nude beach.

DIRECTIONS: The easiest way to get to the beach is to take a taxi or a bus to the Maspalomas Lighthouse at Playa del Faro. From the lighthouse, walk east past the commercial development to the beach (which is marked).

PLAYA DE MATA NEGRA
(HUELVA)

This beach is more of a local gay hangout than an actual nude beach. Nude bathing occurs in the dunes. Be careful about being naked near the water; see what's going on on the rest of the beach first.

DIRECTIONS: From Huelva take Route A497 to the coast. Turn left and head southeast several kilometers toward the town of Punta Umbria. Just before Punta Umbria there is a small forest facing the sea. Park here and walk to the beach.

PLAYAS DEL MUERTO
(SITGES - COSTA DORADO)

Sitges is a popular gay travel destination. These are two adjacent pebbly beaches; the one to the west is almost exclusively gay.

DIRECTIONS: From Sitges, take the train to the stop at Hotel Terramar. On foot, walk west along the railroad tracks. Pass the Terramar golf course and the parking lot for Platja les Coves, and then go behind the filtering station and up the hill to the first bay. Walk across the beach to the second bay to find the gay nude area.

PLAYA SON BOU
(MENORCA)

The island of Menorca is not as popular with gay tourists, but it does have this beach that is used by some gay men.

DIRECTIONS: Follow Route C721 west from Mahon. After about twelve kilometers take the turnoff to the left for Son Bou. About seven kilometers down this road you will find Hotel Sol Milanos. Park in the hotel lot, if you can, and walk to the beach. Look for the rocky headland where nude bathers are found.

PLAYA DE LA TEJITA
(CANARY ISLANDS)

This nude beach on the island of Tenerife is popular with gay men.

DIRECTIONS: From Los Critianos go east on Route TF1 about 10 kilometers, then turn right onto Route TF65 and go toward Los Abrigos. At the coast, go left on Route TF643. Playa de la Tejita is on the right just east of Los Abrigos. The nude section is to the right as you face the water.

PLAYA DE ZARAUTZ
(NEAR SAN SEBASTIAN)

A beautiful beach that sees many crowds. The far end near the golf course is largely nude and attracts gay men.

DIRECTIONS: In Zarautz there are signs for the beach. Once there, the nude section is to the right.

EL TORN
(TARRAGONA)

A large official nude beach that is very popular, but due to the large size of the beach it may not feel too crowded. The beach draws a mixed crowd including gay men.

DIRECTIONS: From Tarragona take Route N340 southwest about 30 kilometers. At kilometer marker 1130, take the turnoff for L'Hospitalet de L'Enfant. The parking lot for the beach is just past the railroad crossing.

ES TRENC
(MALLORCA)

This is an unofficial nude beach on the island of Mallorca, which has an established gay scene. There are food and beverage vendors on the beach and the water is great for swimming.

DIRECTIONS: From the airport near La Palma, go southeast on C717 to Campos. In the center of Campos, turn right on the road toward Sa Rapita and go south about 11 kilometers. Turn left at the sign labeled "Ses Covetes" and go to the T intersection. Go right for one and a half kilometers then turn left onto the beach road. The nude area is between the two snack bars.

VERA PLAYA
(ALMERIA)
Website: www.veraplaya.es

Vera is a naturist resort similar to but smaller than Cap d'Agde in France. There is a hotel, supermarket, bars sports facilities, etc. all for nude use. While this is a naturist, family-oriented resort, it is also visited by many gay men.

DIRECTIONS: Vera is approximately 100 kilometers northeast of Almeria in the vicinity of Mojácar and Garrucha.

SWEDEN

NUDE BEACHES / RECREATION AREAS

FRESCATI
(STOCKHOLM)

A nude beach near the university that is used mostly by gay men.

> *DIRECTIONS:* Take the subway to the Universitetet stop. Walk underneath the overpass, and then go left through the wood toward the water.

LÅNGHOLMEN PARK
(STOCKHOLM)

This park in the city has beach areas that are used for nude sunbathing and are popular with gay men.

> *DIRECTIONS:* Take the subway to the Hornstull stop. Board Bus 54 or 66 and get off at either Högalidsgatan Street or Bergsund Street then go to Västerbron Bridge. The hill above the café is popular with gay men.

SKUTBERGET
(KARLSTAD)

This is a campground and beach popular with a mixture of straight families, couples, and gay men.

> *DIRECTIONS:* From Karlstad, head west on Route E18 a few kilometers and look for signs to Skutberget.

SMITHSKA UDDEN
(GÖTEBORG)

This is a popular clothed beach with nude sections at either end. The crowds in the nude sections are predominantly male.

DIRECTIONS: From Göteborg go south toward Särö. After you pass Särö you will reach Frölunda Torg where you should look for signs for the Näset exit. Take the exit and follow the road to Näset where there will be signs for Smithska Udden. You can also take public transportation to the beach. Take trolley #2 or #3 from Frölunda Torg to Näset, and then take bus 92 to the beach.

SWITZERLAND

NUDE BEACHES / RECREATION AREAS

BERN PUBLIC POOLS
(BERN)

Two of the city's public pools have lawns where nude sunbathing is permitted. These are Lorraine-Freibad and Marzili-Freibad. Both have a gay attendance.

DIRECTIONS: Check Bern phone directory for numbers and directions.

SCHAFFHAUSERRHEINWEG
(BASEL)

This term refers to an area on the Rhine in Basel. There is a section popular for nude sunbathing that is frequented by gay men.

DIRECTIONS: Located between the St. Albans ferry station and the public restrooms on the northern banks of the Rhine River.

WERDININSELI
(ZÜRICH)

This is a nude beach on a small river island in the Limmat River which flows through Zürich. The beach is almost exclusively gay.

DIRECTIONS: Take Tram 4 of Bus 80 or 89 to the Tüffenwies stop. From the stop, walk over the river onto the island and find the big colored while. Walk beyond the wheel to the end of the small island to reach the nude beach.

THAILAND

NUDE BEACHES / RECREATION AREAS

FREEDOM BEACH
(PHUCKET ISLAND)

This beach is accessible only by boat and you should use discretion before disrobing because it is not officially nude. Patong Beach is the popular clothed beach on the island and you'll find Freedom Beach much quieter.

DIRECTIONS: Go to the southern end of Patong Beach and inquire about hiring a longtail boat to take you to Freedom Beach. Keeping with local custom, you should haggle over the price.

UNITED KINGDOM

NUDE CLUBS / GROUPS / ORGANIZATIONS

GYMNOS

BM Box 5147
London, WC 1N 3XX ENGLAND
Contact: Mark or Brian 020-8988 0152
Email: gymnos_naturists@lycos.com
Website: www.gymnos.org

Approx. 400 members
Members-only newsletter
Yearly dues: 18 Pounds Full membership / 8 Pounds swimming-only membership.
Concessions available. Nude swimming on Tuesday and Friday evenings. 2.40
Pounds per session plus 1.50 pounds for non-members.
Unlimited attendance
Potential members welcome
4-5 parties per month (no fee)

NORTHERN GAY NATURISTS (NGN)

PO Box 19
Wakefiled Yorkshire WF 1 2YE United Kingdom

MANCHESTER AREA GAY NATURIST ORGANIZATION (MANGO)

Contact: Christopher (Chris) Jeffery van Ackland
(+64) 9 418 2388
Email: nude_n_manchester@yahoo.co.uk

CLOTHING-OPTIONAL ACCOMMODATIONS

BOCOMBE MILL COTTAGE

Bocombe, Parkham
Bideford, Devon EX39 5PH
United Kingdom
(+44) 1237 451 293
Fax: (+44) 1237 451 293
Email: info@bocombe.co.uk
Website: www.bocombe.co.uk

Rural guesthouse for gay men. 3 rooms (all with private facilities). Pool and ocean nearby. Nudity permitted in garden and orchard. Gourmet country food.

CLIFF HOUSE HOTEL

St Marks Rd
Meadfoot Beach
Torquay, Devon TQ1 2EH
England
(+44) 1803 294 656
(+44) 1803 211 983
Email: cliffhouse@talktalk.net
Website: www.cliffhousehotel.co.uk

The Cliff House Hotel is gay-owned and provides a service in relaxed surroundings; offering that "Home from Home" atmosphere. Celebrating its 38th year.

NUDE BEACHES / RECREATION AREAS

BLACKGANG BEACH
(ISLE OF WIGHT)

The beach can draw several nude users on good days and is popular with gay men.

DIRECTIONS: Take an auto ferry from Portsmouth or Southampton. Take Route A3055 southwest around the island toward Chale and St. Catherine's lighthouse. Look for Sandrock Road and park in the small lot at the end of the road. Take the path at Rocken End headland to get to the beach.

BRIGHTON BEACH
(BRIGHTON)

This beach has an official nude zone. Take in some of the amusement fairs and parks in Brighton while visiting.

DIRECTIONS: Take the train from London. The nude beach is located between Peter Pan's Playground and the large marina just east of the main promenade.

CORTON SANDS — AKA GUNTON SANDS
(NEAR LOWESTOFT)

This beach is designated nude and attracts a mixed crowd.

DIRECTIONS: Take Route A12 north from Lowestoft, then go right on Route B1385. Look for Tramps Alley opposite Pleasurewood Hills Theme Park. Park at Tramps Alley and go to the left as you face the water. You will reach the nude area after about 200 yards.

FRAISTHORPE BEACH
(NEAR BRIDLINGTON)

On nice summer days this beach can see many visitors with a decent number of gay men.

>   *DIRECTIONS:* Bridlington is east of Leeds and York and northeast of Hull. Parking is available in two pay lots off Route A165 at Fraisthorpe Picnic Site of a few miles farther south at the lot in Barmston village. From the Fraisthorpe Picnic Site, walk to the right as you face the water about one mile. The second concrete gun bunker is generally the beginning of the nude section.

HOLKHAM HALL BEACH
(NEAR WELLS-NEXT-THE-SEA)

This beach is part of the Holkham Hall Estate and the owner permits nude use. A beach patrolman is employed to keep the dunes free of cruising activity. The beach draws a mixed crowd.

>   *DIRECTIONS:* Take Route A149 west of Wells-next-the Sea and look for Holkham Hall Estate. Turn right onto Lady Anne Road opposite the estate gates and park in the lot (fee charged). There is a map on the board at the lot that points the way to the nude area.

HORSEY BEACH/WINTERTON DUNES
(HORSEY)

This beach has a distinct gay area. You can reach it from Horsey or from the Winterton Dunes nature reserve.

>   *DIRECTIONS:* Take Route B1159 north from Great Yarmouth to Horsey. Park in the lot at Horsey Reserve. Walk to the right as you face the water. Nude use occurs in the two miles south of the parking lot. You can park at Winterton Dunes and walk north if you wish. When you pass the second large gap in the sea wall you are in the gay section.

KINSHALDY BEACH
(NEAR LEUCHARS, SCOTLAND)

This beach has a few areas used by nudists with a popular section used by gay men.

> DIRECTIONS: Park in the Forestry Commission pay lot. This beach is well marked with signs. To reach the gay area, walk to the left on the beach about three quarters of a mile from the main beach.

MORFA DYFFRYN BEACH
(NEAR HARLECH, WALES)

A very popular nude beach in Wales that will see hundreds of users on peak summer days. The beach is popular with gay men.

> DIRECTIONS: Take Route A496 south form Harlech. In Dyffryn Ardudwy village, look for a big sign advertising Benar Beach Camp Site, then take the next road to the right and go to the parking lot by the Benar Beach camping area. Walk to the right as you face the water for about 20 minutes to reach the nude area.

PETITOR BEACH
(NEAR TORQUAY)

A pebble beach that is popular with gay men.

> DIRECTIONS: From central Torquay, go north on the main highway to Petitor Road. Park on the side of the road, walk to the end, through the gate, and down the steep hill of grass. At the bottom of the hill there are steps to the right that lead to a clothed beach. Instead of taking the stairs, take the path to the left which will take you directly to the nude area. The gay section is to the left.

PORTSLADE BEACH
(NEAR BRIGHTON)

This beach is more private than Brighton Beach and attracts fewer gawkers. It is located only about 4 miles from Brighton Beach.

> DIRECTIONS: Take Route A259 west from Brighton to Hove. Look for Port of Call Pub. Turn left and follow Basin Road South; the road will turn and follow a wall that separates the road from the beach. Park near lamp post 77 and walk to the west end of the beach.

ST. OSYTH BEACH
(NEAR CLACTON)

This beach is close to London and popular with a mixed crowd of nudists including gay men. Gay men tend to gather at the far end near the fence.

DIRECTIONS: Take Route B1027 from Colchester to the village of St. Osyth and follow signs to Hutleys caravan park. Pay the parking fee at the kiosk and turn right to follow the beach road to the parking area. This parking area is actually in the nude area, so you can disrobe in your car if you wish.

STUDLAND BEACH
(NEAR BOURNEMOUTH)

There is a marked section of this beach for nude use. If you are nude beyond the posted area, you will be asked by patrollers to move to the nude section. The dunes can be cruisy, but beach patrols are frequent.

DIRECTIONS: From Wareham take A351 south to Corfe Castle, then bear left onto B3351 to the town of Studland. Drive through the village to the ferry. If you can find parking near the ferry, you can hike to the nude beach. Auto and passenger ferries go to the beach from the town of Sandbanks.